Leader's Guide

WALK THE TALK
In the Steps of the Soul Man

FAITH in Motion

Jim Still-Pepper

Abingdon Press

WALK THE TALK
In the Steps of the Soul Man

LEADER'S GUIDE

Copyright © 2003 by Abingdon Press.

All rights reserved.

With the exception of those items so noted, no part of this work may be reproduced or transmitted in any form or by any means, electronic or mechanical, including photocopying and recording, or by any information storage or retrieval system, except as may be expressly permitted by the 1976 Copyright Act or in writing from the publisher. Requests for permission should be addressed to Abingdon Press, 201 Eighth Avenue, South, P.O. Box 801, Nashville, TN 37202-0801.

This book is printed on acid-free, recycled paper.

Unless otherwise noted, Scripture quotations are from the *New Revised Standard Version of the Bible,* copyright © 1989, Division of Christian Education of the National Council of the Churches of Christ in the United States of America. Used by permission. All rights reserved.

MANUFACTURED IN THE UNITED STATES OF AMERICA

Development Team
Jola Bortner
Rusty Cartee
Harriette Cross
Tim Gossett
Sharon Meads
Beth Miller
David Stewart

Editorial Team
Tim Gossett, Development Editor
Sheila K. Hewitt, Production Editor

Design Team
Keely J. Moore, Design Manager
Kelly Chinn, Designer

Administrative Staff
Neil M. Alexander, Publisher
Harriett Jane Olson, Vice President/Editor of Church School Resources
Bob Shell, Director of Youth Resources

04 05 06 07 08 09 10 11 12—10 9 8 7 6 5 4 3 2

Contents

Session 1: Walk Humbly 7

Session 2: Walk in Love 13

Session 3: Walk in the Light 19

Session 4: Walk in Darkness 25

Session 5: Walk to Emmaus 31

Session 6: Walk as He Walked 37

Session 7: Walk in Newness of Life 43

Reproducible Pages 49

A Walking Retreat 57

Out and About: Walking for Jesus 62

Worship Service: Walk in God's Ways 63

How to Use Faith in Motion

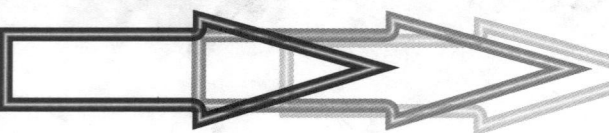

Leader Guide Information and Formation

Topic and Key Verse
This Life-to-Bible curriculum starts with important topics for junior highs and goes to God's Word.

Take-Home Learning
The goal for the session is clear.

Younger Youth and the Topic
Find out more about your youth and how they are likely to connect with this concern.

Theology and the Topic
How does Christian faith and tradition help us to understand and deal with the concern?

You and the Scripture
Our being formed as a Christian through Bible reflection and prayer is essential for our teaching.

Transformation

The Ultimate Goal:
Youth will become more fully devoted disciples of Jesus Christ.

Overview Chart
Look here for the big picture of the session. Also note the key activities, just in case time is tight.

Get Ready
The opening activity engages youth as they arrive.

Jump In
Learning activities give youth a common base for making new connections.

Look for Life
What do the Scriptures have to say? What does this mean for my life? What is a Christian to do?

Go With God
The learnings are not just for Sunday! Ritual and mystery, prayer and commitment change hearts.

Student Journal and Reproducible Handouts

Life Focus
Topics deal with issues and concerns important to junior high youth.

Spirit Forming
The journal provides practical help and scriptural encouragement.

Group Friendly
Printed Scripture references, discussion questions, and handouts facilitate participation by individuals and small groups.

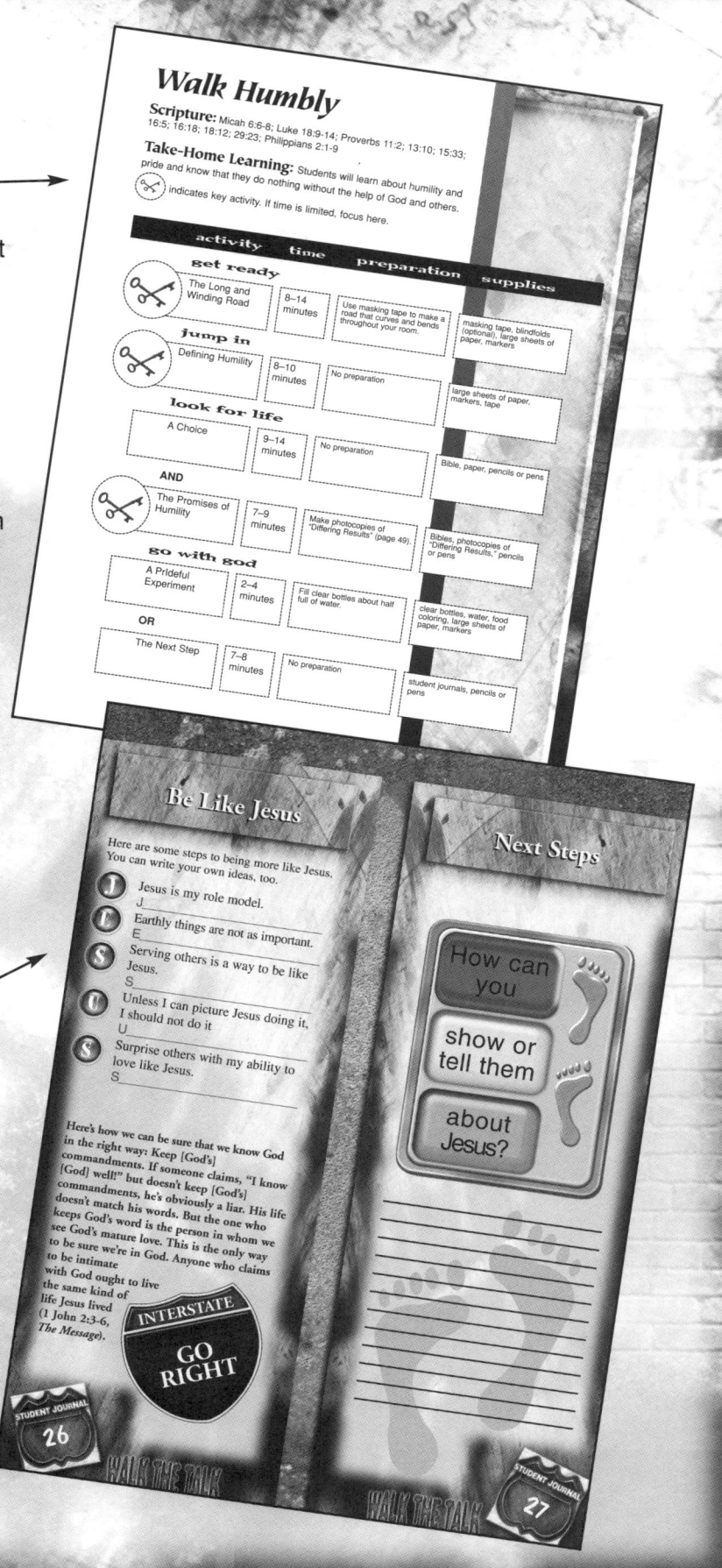

Are You Walking Your Talk?

Many elements make up a great Sunday school class—an inviting atmosphere; appealing curriculum; and of course, chocolate-frosted donuts. Undoubtedly, though, the most important faith-building element of the classroom is you. The youth in your class look to you for help in making sense of God, the world, and the Bible. That can be a pretty scary reality.

Fortunately, you love teenagers. That's obvious, or you wouldn't be teaching this class. Yet youth need to see in you more than just a person who doesn't mind being around them for an hour or so each week. They look to you to see a realistic example of what it means to be a Christian. They want to find in you someone walking the talk—really living the things you teach. Walking is a whole body endeavor (if you doubt that, try walking a block without moving your upper body and using your eyes and ears). Like walking, the life of faith is a whole-body experience. Walk and talk need to go together.

- *When you look at the world, do you see everyone as a child of God? Do you see your fellow church members as the body of Christ in the world today?*

- *If you listen to people's conversations at work, can you hear their yearnings, emotions, and needs? Are the shouts of children on a playground and the chirping of a cricket like an ever-present chorus of praise, or are they noisy distractions and annoyances?*

- *Does your diet reflect your faith? Do you treat your body as the temple of the Holy Spirit that it is? Do the things you eat cause harm to God's creation?*

- *What fills up your mind? If one of your youth unexpectedly dropped by your home, what would he or she find you watching on TV. Why? Think about the last three books you read for pleasure. What would they indicate about your values, your passions, and your faith?*

Just as our bodies need regular exercise so our muscles don't atrophy and our health stays strong, our faith needs to be regularly exercised so that it strengthens and maintains us. So go on—get walking! Be sure to ask your youth to walk with you.

1

Walk Humbly

Topic: Humility of faith

Scriptures: Micah 6:6-8; Luke 18:9-14; Proverbs 11:2; 13:10; 15:33; 16:5; 16:18; 18:12; 29:23; Philippians 2:1-9

Key Verse: He has told you, O mortal, what is good; and what does the LORD require of you but to do justice, and to love kindness, and to walk humbly with your God? (Micah 6:8)

Take-Home Learning: Students will learn about humility and pride and know that they do nothing without the help of God and others.

Younger Youth and the Topic

Humility is a difficult concept for many younger youth to grasp and practice. Their tendency to focus on and differentiate themselves from their peers can interfere with their ability to live humbly. Youth also may think that being humble means that they can't take pride in their accomplishments or that they must be a doormat that others can walk over. Help them see that they can be proud of themselves while knowing that it is only through the help of others and of God that we do anything.

The opposite of Christian humility is spiritual pride, a belief that our actions and our faith should impress others. One way youth sometimes struggle with spiritual pride is by feeling as if they should be recognized or rewarded for the good deeds they do in service to others. In addition, they may feel self-righteous when they believe that the adults around them are not serving others. Help the youth to see that pride is sinful when it is based on pushing someone else down through actions, words, or attitudes.

Younger youth often look for a cause or a purpose for their lives. This issue can tap that need—walking the talk is a tremendous purpose for living. Watch for youth struggling to put their faith into action; many will not have the humility to admit to you their faith-related difficulties. A variety of reasons cause youth to struggle with walking the talk, including poor self-esteem, no motivation to change their faith, feeling uncomfortable with change, peer or family pressure, lack of support or community, sin.

Identifying the barriers is a first step to helping youth work through them. Once you or the youth have identified any barriers, the youth will be in a better position to overcome them. In addition, we must continually work to surround youth with a community that loves and supports them—even through their mistakes, questions of faith, and growing pains.

Walk Humbly

Read **Micah 6:6-8.**

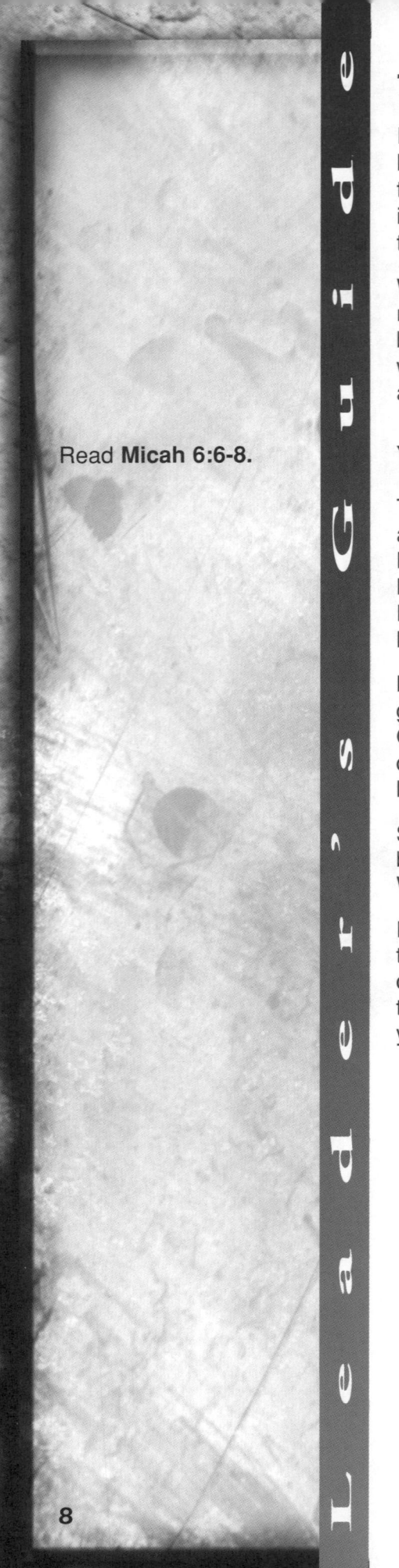

Theology and the Topic

Is humility something we achieve? Is it a gift from God? Is it a result of a life of seeking God in all things? Just how is a humble person supposed to act, anyway? If we think that we're being humble, can we really say it? The answers to these questions are elusive as we read the Bible, but the Scripture clearly calls us to be humble.

While defining *humility* can be hard, knowing why we are to be humble is much easier. We are to be humble because we really have nothing to boast about. Without God, we are nothing. God has given us everything we have, and God has created us to be who we are. How can we be anything but humble in the face of this truth?

You and the Scripture

The prophet Micah puts in simple form an answer to a question we all ask about our faith: "Just what does God want me to do, anyway?" Micah's answer is one of action: Do! Love! Walk! In one verse, Micah has summarized the teachings of Amos (God desires righteousness), Hosea (God desires steadfast love), and Isaiah (God desires faith and humility).

Many times during this series, you are going to be challenging youth to give up or to take on something in order to gain a closer relationship with God and to be a better witness in the world. But what about you? What do you need to give up? What is distracting you from your walk? Make a list of things that may be hindering your walk and relationship with God.

Some very practical things to consider giving up are things that lead to burnout or activities that distract you. What could enhance your walk? What things can make your witness more compelling?

Do not feel obligated to add more to your "to-do" list. However, it is often the case that change comes about only when we are challenged to live differently. Walking the talk begins when you look inward at yourself and then ask God to lead you forward. Once you have taken this first step, you will be more fully ready to challenge your youth.

Walk the Talk: In the Steps of the Soul Man

Walk Humbly

Scripture: Micah 6:6-8; Luke 18:9-14; Proverbs 11:2; 13:10; 15:33; 16:5; 16:18; 18:12; 29:23; Philippians 2:1-9

Take-Home Learning: Students will learn about humility and pride and know that they do nothing without the help of God and others.

🗝 indicates key activity. If time is limited, focus here.

activity	time	preparation	supplies
get ready			
🗝 The Long and Winding Road	8–14 minutes	Use masking tape to make a road that curves and bends throughout your room.	masking tape, blindfolds (optional), large sheets of paper, markers
jump in			
🗝 Defining Humility	8–10 minutes	No preparation	large sheets of paper, markers, tape
look for life			
A Choice	9–14 minutes	No preparation	Bible, paper, pencils or pens
AND			
🗝 The Promises of Humility	7–9 minutes	Make photocopies of "Differing Results" (page 49).	Bibles, photocopies of "Differing Results," pencils or pens
go with god			
A Prideful Experiment	2–4 minutes	Fill clear bottles about half full of water.	clear bottles, water, food coloring, large sheets of paper, markers
OR			
The Next Step	7–8 minutes	No preparation	student journals, pencils or pens

get ready

Supplies: masking tape, blindfolds (optional), large sheets of paper, markers, Bible

Before class, use masking tape to make a road that curves and bends throughout your room (and, if possible, the hallway outside your room). The tape should mark both sides of the road, and there should just be enough space between the sides of the tape to put a foot in.

Teacher Tip: Have a few adults or youth walk around to make sure no one gets hurt during the activity.

If you have time, let the youth switch places and do the activity again.

jump in

Supplies: large sheets of paper, markers, tape

Teacher Tip: Refer the youth to page 6 of the student journal if they need help with this assignment.

The Long and Winding Road (8–14 minutes)

As students arrive, engage them in conversation about driving. If you have youth who are already driving, ask for volunteers to talk about how much they do or don't like driving. Ask those who don't drive yet to talk about what they are looking forward to most about driving.

Say: "When you start driving, you have a guide who can help you to watch the road and stay on course. I'd like for you to work together to navigate this road. Choose partners—one person to be the leader and one person who will walk the road with his or her eyes closed. The leader should guide his or her partner through the road with voice only—no touching."

If you have blindfolds, hand them out. Have pairs begin at the starting line one at a time. Once a pair has started, the next pair can then begin.

After a few minutes, call time, even if all the groups have not had a chance to get to the end. Have the youth sit down where they are. The blindfolded people can remove their blindfolds.

Ask those who were blindfolded:

- What was it like to be blind?
- Did you like having to be led? Why, or why not?
- What made it hard to follow your leader's directions?

Ask those who were leaders:

- How hard was it to lead?
- Did you like having the responsibility of leading? Why, or why not?
- How were you trying to help your blind person? (Record these answers on large paper.)

Say: "God has a road, a way for each of us. Throughout this series, Walk the Talk, you will be challenged to walk in God's way. God's way is sometimes more difficult than other ways and sometimes easier, but it is always the best way for us to go. It is the best way to go, because God wants what is best for us. Today we talking about walking humbly—or with humility." Read Micah 6:6-8 aloud.

Defining Humility (8–10 minutes)

Designate up to six groups (or individuals). Assign one or more of these:

- Define the word *pride* as a positive quality.
- Define the word *pride* as a negative quality.
- Define the word *humble* as a positive trait.
- Define the word *humble* as a negative trait.
- Give examples of persons who are full of pride—both positive and negative (no names).
- Give examples of persons who are humble—both positive and negative (no names).

Walk the Talk: In the Steps of the Soul Man

Say: "You may use words, images, actions, skits, or whatever method you'd like to complete your definition or describe your examples."

Hand out large sheets of paper and markers to each group. Give the groups 2–4 minutes to come up with their definitions, lists, and so on. Bring the groups back together and have them report. Post the papers on pride on one wall, and post the ones on humility on the opposite wall.

Ask:

- What's the difference between being proud of oneself and being prideful?

A Choice (9–14 minutes)

Say: "As with most roads, there are always choices to be made on God's road. Let's read about the choice Jesus gives us regarding humility."

Invite a youth to read aloud Luke 18:9-14.

Divide the class into groups of three, and ask them to create a modern day skit using the story line from this parable. Give the youth about three minutes to be creative, then let them present their skits.

Ask these questions:

- Why would a person become prideful?
- Why might a person choose to be humble?
- What things make it easy to be too proud?
- What things make it easy to be humble?
- What do you think Jesus meant by saying that the humble would be exalted and those who exalted themselves would be humbled?
- What else has Jesus said at the end of other stories that is similar to this statement? *(The first shall be last; the last shall be first in the kingdom of God.)*

Read aloud the following translation of Luke 18:14:

> Jesus commented, "This tax man, not the other, went home made right with God. If you walk around with your nose in the air, you're going to end up flat on your face, but if you're content to be simply yourself, you will become more than yourself" (*The Message*).

Ask:

- What do you think it means to be "content to simply be yourself"?

AND

The Promises of Humility (7–9 minutes)

Say: "Humility improves our relationship with others and with God, whereas pride is often hurts our relationships. The Book of Proverbs has a lot to say about pride and humility. Let's take a look at these proverbs."

Walk Humbly

look for life

Supplies: Bible, paper, pens or pencils

Optional: During this activity, take time to listen together to the song "The Walk," from *Signs of Life*, by Steven Curtis Chapman.

Teacher Tip: An alternative starter to this discussion is the activity on page 5 of the student journal.

Supplies: Bibles, copies of "Differing Results" (page 49), pens or pencils

Differing Results
(answer key)

Answers will depend on the Bible translation used.

- 11:2—Wisdom, Disgrace
- 13:10—Listens to advice, Quarreling
- 15:33—Honor
- 16:5—Punishment
- 16:18—Destruction
- 18:12—Honor, Downfall
- 29:23—Honor, Humiliation

go with god

Supplies: two clear bottles, water, food coloring, large sheets of paper, markers

Supplies: student journals, pens or pencils

A song that contains the words from Micah 6:8 is Jim Strathdee's beautiful round "What Does the Lord Require of You?" from the cassette *Jubilee,* which can be ordered from www.strathdeemusic.com/toc.htm.

Divide the youth into pairs (or threes). Hand out copies of "Differing Results" (page 49). Say: "With your partner(s), look up the Scripture and fill in the chart. You won't have an answer under both columns for every passage."

Give the pairs a few minutes to work. Then say: "Proverbs are meant to be memorized so that they'll come to mind at just the right moment. With your partner, pick one of these proverbs that speaks to you. Practice reciting it to each another until you can recite it from memory."

A Prideful Experiment (2–4 minutes)

Fill two clear glass bottles, jars, or vases about half full with water. Say: "Imagine that you are the water in these containers, and the food coloring is your pride." (Pour a few drops of color into the water of one.)

Ask:

- What has happened?
- In what ways can pride affect us similarly to how the food coloring affected the water?" (*It can "color" or seep into all of our attitudes and behavior.*)

Say: "Now imagine that the second bottle is God's Spirit. It is clean, clear, and pure. God wants to fill you." (Pour the pure water into the bottle of colored water.)

Ask:

- What happened to the pure water? (*It is absorbed.*)
- What happened to the colored water?" (*It is gradually diluted.*)
- How is this example similar to what happens to us when we allow God's Spirit into our lives? (*Our pride weakens, but it doesn't disappear completely due to our human nature.*)
- Why doesn't God like pride?
- We talked about this earlier—What's the difference between being proud of yourself and being prideful?

On a large sheet of paper, write the word *pride,* capitalizing the "i" to make it stand out. Ask: "When I write the word this way, what does this remind us about pride?" (*Pride is putting oneself before God.*)

OR

The Next Step (7–8 minutes)

Hand out the student journals. Play some soft music in the background. Direct the students to pages 4–7 and ask them to follow the directions.

After they have worked on their journals, gather the class together. If you know a song that contains the words from Micah 6:8, sing it together. Otherwise, read the verse a phrase at a time and have the youth repeat it. Then together say the verse from memory.

Walk the Talk: In the Steps of the Soul Man

Walk in Love

Topic: How faith has an impact on others

Scripture: Romans 14:1-21; 1 John 4:19-21

Key Verse: "If your brother or sister is being injured by what you eat, you are no longer walking in love" (Romans 14:15).

Take-Home Learning: Our faith must never cause someone else to stumble in his or hers.

Younger Youth and the Topic

Teenagers are pretty adept at spotting a phony. They've figured out that people aren't always trustworthy, that adults sometimes lie to them, and that many people often say one thing but do the opposite. Often teens will refuse to abide by their parents' wishes because they see these instructions as hypocritical, such as when parents tell their sons or daughters that they should not waste their money on video games while the parents "waste" their money on coffee, hobbies, or fancy landscaping. Younger youth believe that hypocrisy is all around them—including among church members. Youth notice that actions and beliefs don't always match up in the lives of many Christians.

However, like most of us, younger youth are not very adept at noticing or confronting hypocrisy in their own lives. Change does not come easily for many of them. Yet their heightened sense of idealism can be the catalyst that leads to a dynamic and vibrant faith. Younger youth are in a great position to wrestle with what it means to walk their talk all the time. They are capable of walking in love. That doesn't mean that they'll be perfect, but they can begin to make steps toward a love-filled faith.

Theology and the Topic

Volumes have been written about love, the most important of the three Christian virtues (along with faith and hope.) Most likely, you and your class have heard many sermons extolling love. Yet many Christians still don't understand this most basic of theological concepts. Far worse, many people outside the church see Christians as some of the most unloving people they know. So just what does it really mean to walk in love?

Perhaps a simple—and yet profoundly difficult—way to understand and practice Christian love is to have equal regard for all of God's creatures. God loves everyone equally; and, therefore, so should we. To walk in love

Walk in Love

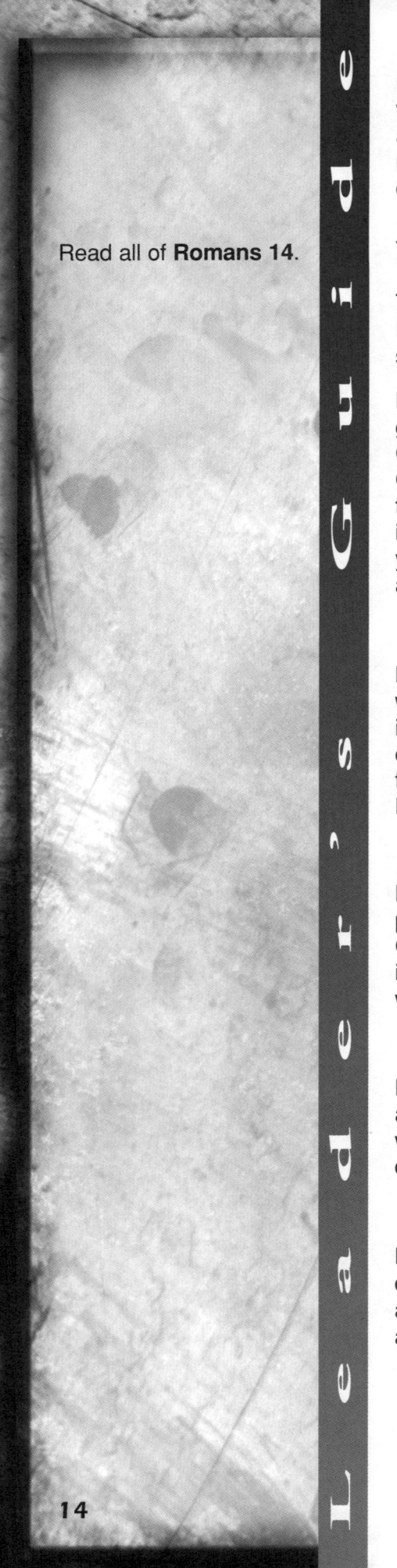

is to recognize and experience our kinship with one another. Seen in this way, love becomes far more than a feeling or even a nice thing done for another person. It's an act of our will—we show compassion to everyone unreservedly. It is also an act of our heart—we value both ourselves and others unconditionally.

You and the Scripture

This week, you'll help youth understand a relatively difficult chapter from Romans. Although the youth won't read the entire chapter, you should be sure to read all of Romans 14 in preparation for this lesson.

Romans 14:1-4—Several times in the New Testament we are given a glimpse of the tensions between Gentile and Jewish converts to Christianity. Examples can be found in Mark 2:13-28; Acts 10:9-16; and Galatians 2:11-14—to name a few. Paul was concerned about these tensions over such matters as diet, because they were creating discord in the Christian community. What are the similar tensions that exist in your faith community? How is Paul's instruction to the Romans useful advice for your church?

Romans 14:5-9—Another disagreement in the early church was over which day should be considered holy. Paul stressed that all Christians can, in their own way, "live in honor of the Lord" as long as their practices are done with this in mind. What in your daily life—eating, work, time with family, leisure activities—might you need to change to make it honor the Lord?

Romans 14:10-13—Paul urged the readers of the letter to never, ever put a barrier between someone else and his or her relationship with Christ. Are there behaviors, attitudes, or even physical barriers that exist in your church or in your life that could be stumbling blocks for people who are new to the faith?

Romans 14:14-19—We are to work for mutual upbuilding and to regard all persons equally. Doing these two things is a key sign that we are walking in love. Are there relationships in your life in which you have a difficult time seeking peace and mutual growth in love?

Romans 14:20-23—Our faith must never lead to another's violation of conscience, and we should not encourage others to act in ways that go against their convictions. What faith convictions held by other Christians are hardest for you to accept as true?

Read all of **Romans 14**.

Leader's Guide

Walk the Talk

Walk in Love

Scripture: Romans 14:1-23; 1 John 4:19-21

Take-Home Learning: Our faith must never cause someone else to stumble in his or hers.

🗝️ indicates key activity. If time is limited, focus here.

activity	time	preparation	supplies

get ready

🗝️ Classic Hypocrite	6–10 minutes	No preparation	paper, pens or pencils

jump in

🗝️ Blocked	9–13 minutes	No preparation	Decks of cards

AND

Roadblocks	6–12 minutes	Write the word *roadblock* on a block of wood.	block of wood

look for life

🗝️ It's Not Just About Food	6–8 minutes	No preparation	Bibles

AND

Who's Watching You?	5–7 minutes	No preparation	large sheets of paper, markers

go with god

The Next Step	5–7 minutes	No preparation	student journals, pens or pencils

get ready

Supplies: paper, pens or pencils

jump in

Supplies: decks of cards

If you don't have enough decks for everyone, call the youth and ask them to bring a few decks of cards to class. Alternatively, put the word out to congregation a week in advance and you'll get many donated decks.

Teacher Tip: Demonstrate the way to lay the cards down as you explain the rules.

Classic Hypocrite (6–10 minutes)

As the youth arrive, have them form groups of two or three. Ask them to make up a short skit about someone who is acting or talking hypocritically. If they get stuck and can't think of an idea, suggest one of the following:

- Parents tell their children not to smoke, but they do.
- A teacher emphasizes fairness in gym class but doesn't give equal opportunity to all players during school basketball games.
- The school uses disposable dishes in the lunch room but has a big emphasis in the classroom on living "green."

After everyone has arrived, have the groups present their skits. It's not crucial that every latecomer be involved in a skit.

Ask:

- When have you experienced someone as a hypocrite? (*no names*)
- Who would you say you're most likely to see as hypocritical—a friend, a parent, or another adult? Why?

Blocked (9–13 minutes)

Give each person a deck of cards (without the jokers). Pair up everyone and have them sit about five feet apart on the floor or at opposite ends of a table. Shuffle the cards well.

Say: "This game is called Blocked. The object of the game is to be the first one to put one suit of cards in order from ace to king. Place your deck face down and turn over one card at a time. When you come to an ace (the suit to build on), begin a stack. Continue turning over cards until you find the "2" of that suit. Place it above the ace; build toward your partner. Continue until you reach the king."

Play once to make sure that everyone understands the game, then ask the youth to reshuffle their cards.

Say: "Now, we're going to change the rules. Each of you has four jacks, one of which you'll need to complete your suit. The other three can be used to block the other person. If you come across a jack of the same color as your opponent's suit, you may place it horizontally at the top of his or her line. He or she must then start over. However, your opponent gets to keep your jack and potentially use it later against you or in his or her own line. So think carefully about using your blocks—they could come back to haunt you later."

Play the game again. After 3–4 minutes, stop the game.

Ask:

- How many of you used your block cards? Why?
- How much harder was it to win the game the second time we played it?

AND

Walk the Talk

Roadblocks (6–12 minutes)

Say: "Think of a time when someone has put a roadblock in your life that made it hard to do something you wanted to do. (Tell your own example.) I'm going to toss the block to someone else to share a story." After all who wish to have spoken, ask:

- How does it feel to have someone place a roadblock in your way?
- In what ways can those blocks be a good thing? (*Because people are looking out for our best interests; roadblocks might prevent us from harming ourselves; they challenge us to work harder for what we want.*)
- In what ways can putting a block in someone's way be harmful? (*If it's done out of selfishness, jealousy, or anger, it might not really be something that is good for them; sometimes excess rules just slow us down and don't serve much purpose.*)
- Can you think of a way a person's behavior could be a stumbling block to others? (*A parent who spends the family income on gambling; a coach who never encourages the weaker players on the team; a friend who pressures others to smoke, drink, be sexually active*)

It's Not Just About Food (6–8 minutes)

Say: "In Paul's time, Christians who had once been Jewish and Christians who had been Gentiles had differences of opinion about the ways they should practice their faith and what traditions, rituals, and rules they should keep. Some Christians, because of their Jewish background, thought that it was important to avoid eating certain kinds of meat, while most Gentile Christians had no problem with it. This was just one disagreement that resulted in mutual dislike and tension within the Christian community. In fact, the people who ate meat called those who didn't 'weak in faith' because they kept following Jewish dietary law."

Hand out Bibles and direct the students to Romans 14. Divide the youth into two groups. Say to the first group: "You are going to be the Jewish Christians, the ones who will not eat certain things because of your religious background." Say to the second group: "You are going to be the Gentile Christians, the ones who eat whatever they choose." Have the a volunteer ("Paul") stand between them and read Romans 14:1-4.

Ask the second group:

- What does Paul say you're supposed to do or not do? (Don't judge one another.)

Ask the first group:

- Why does Paul say you should avoid criticizing the other group?" (*God welcomes both.*)

Have another volunteer "Paul" read Romans 14:13-15. Ask the first group:

- What was the stumbling block that Paul was talking about that the other group put in your way? (*Calling you weak in faith because of your diet.*)

Walk in Love

Supplies; block of wood

Before class, find a block of wood and write the word *roadblock* on it in bold letters. Think of a story from your life when you faced a "roadblock" placed by others in your path.

look for life

Supplies: Bibles

Ask the second group:

- How do you know whether you have stopped walking in love? (*Because you do something that offends or hurts or leads other Christians to sin.*)

Ask both groups:

- What does it mean to "cause the ruin of one for whom Christ died"? (*To turn them away from Christ because of your actions.*)

Have the first "Paul" read Romans 14:17-21. Ask:

- In the end, what does Paul think people should do when it comes to diet? (*Don't do anything that would cause a fellow Christian to stumble.*)

Ask:

- Do you think that this advice could apply to other behaviors besides eating? Can you name some examples? (*If they have difficulty making this connection, write on a large sheet of paper the following words:* music, movies, friends, your words, drinking, putting down or ignoring *persons.*)
- If you had friends who were new Christians or not one at all, how could any of these be a stumbling block that might turn them away from Christ?

AND

Who's Watching You? (5–7 minutes)

Divide into three groups of at least two people. Ask one group to list ways people watch or keep track of someone's behavior. Ask the second to list people who typically pay attention to their behavior in a day. Ask the third group to list actions or words they wouldn't do or say around a pastor or youth leader that they might do or say around friends. Have each group present their lists.

Ask:

- How does it make you feel to know that people are always watching you?
- Why are we less likely to do certain things around some people?"
- If we took Paul's message seriously—that if we do anything that could turn someone away from Christ we are not walking in love—how would our behavior change?"
- "In what ways do people look to our actions and words to see what Christians are like? What happens if they don't see much of a difference between us and other people?"

The Next Step (5–7 minutes)

Hand out the student journals and pens. Play some quiet music in the background to help the youth relax and focus. Give everyone about five minutes to do pages 8–11, then collect the journals.

Have the group form a circle. End by reading to each other Romans 15:5-6. Start with one person who blesses the person to the right, and then continue around the circle until everyone has blessed a classmate.

Walk the Talk

Supplies: large sheets of paper, markers

look for life

Supplies: student journals, pens or pencils

3

Walk in the Light

Topic: Being the light of Christ in the world

Scripture: John 8:12-20

Key Verse: "Again Jesus spoke to them, saying, 'I am the light of the world. Whoever follows me will never walk in darkness but will have the light of life'" (John 8:12).

Take-Home Learning: To walk in the light of Christ is to be a follower of Jesus and to reflect his light to others.

Younger Youth and the Topic

For those of us who walk in the light regularly, it may be hard to understand people who avoid or almost seem afraid of the light of Christ. Increase your understanding of people who struggle with light by trying the following experiment:

Sit in a dark room for about five minutes. (The darker the room is, the more you will understand.) Keep your eyes open. Try seeing as much as you can during your five minutes. After five minutes have passed, turn on all the bright lights you can.

How did you react?

Most of us pull away and hide our eyes. This is the same reaction many youth have to the message of Jesus Christ. They pull away, hide their eyes, and appear content with darkness. The dark calls them, lulls them, soothes them with an eerie comfort.

For some of the youth in your class, living in the light is a radical change from the way they have lived before. Others may be trying hard to live in the light but have many friends or family members who do not. Changing direction is never easy. Some people, such as Saul on the road to Damascus, need a strong change to propel them onward. Other people, such as Moses, need to be convinced over time. Moses needed the burning bush, the serpent-staff, and Aaron, among other signs, before he was ready to move ahead.

Youth are no different. Think about the teenagers you know. Which of them can handle a strong change and are ready to boldly live in the light?

Which of your youth are struggling with what it means to live in the light and, perhaps, will change at a slower pace?

Walk in the Light

Read **John 8:12-20.**

Session Preparation

Before class, turn off all of the lights and cover up the windows to make your meeting room as dark as possible. Place candles (ones that cannot be easily tipped over) around the room or plug in night-lights which can illuminate the space.

Before class, gather some inexpensive flashlights and batteries, preferably ones that will come apart into several pieces. Take out the batteries and remove the light bulb, lens cap, switch, and so forth. Place the pieces from each flashlight into a separate plastic bag.

Leader's Guide

Theology and the Topic

Light would have little meaning if we did not also experience darkness. But, of course, we do. In fact, living in darkness is our natural state. Our cry is for God to provide light for our walk. Jesus, who not only shows us the light but is himself the light of the world, makes our world bright and enables us to see the darkness around us. Because of Jesus, we do not simply grope about in the dark but see the way—his way.

However, simply seeing a brighter path is not enough. We are called to walk in the light, to be *followers* and not just *admirers* of Jesus. Following implies relationship; indeed, when God calls us out of darkness, God calls us into relationship with God, with one another, and with all of creation.

You and the Scripture

The conversations Jesus had with the Pharisees in John 7 and 8 were probably originally connected, with the story of the woman caught in adultery being added later. Both of these chapters are set during the end of the Feast of Tabernacles (also known as the Feast of Booths), one of the most important Jewish festivals. The festival was a reminder of God's saving presence in the past and God's promises for the future. A major reason for this festival was to commemorate God's gift of water which flowed from the rock in the desert when the Israelites were wandering in the wilderness (Numbers 20:2-13). Jesus refers to this story in John 7:37 ("Let anyone who is thirsty come to me. . . .")

Now, in John 8:12-20, Jesus uses one of the other symbols of the Feast: light. During this time, large golden lamps brightened the Temple court. Now, Jesus refers to himself as a light to be followed, hearkening back to the story of the pillar of light which led the Israelites in the wilderness. For the gospel writer, Jesus leads us through the darkness into the light of God.

How has Jesus been a light that leads you in times of darkness?

As a teacher, you reflect the light of Christ to your students. Try this breath prayer to center yourself before class. Sit comfortably, and relax your breathing. With each breath, say these words to yourself: "May I reflect your light, O Christ."

Repeat this phrase for several minutes as your prayer for today's session.

Walk the Talk

Walk in the Light

Scripture: John 8:12-20

Take-Home Learning: To walk in the light of Christ is to be a follower of Jesus and to reflect his light to others.

(key icon) indicates key activity. If time is limited, focus here.

activity	time	preparation	supplies
get ready			
Without Light (key)	5–8 minutes	Take the flashlights apart and put the parts to each one and their batteries in separate bags.	flashlights, plastic bags, night-lights or candles and matches
jump in			
Talking About Light and Darkness	7–8 minutes	Use masking tape to make a road that curves and bends throughout your room.	large sheets of paper, markers, tape
look for life			
A Faith Trial (key)	10–15 minutes	No Preparation	Bibles
AND			
Sharing Your Story	7–10 minutes	No preparation	None
go with god			
I See Your Light	4–10 minutes	Entitle a sheet of paper "I See Your Light." Leave space to write a name. Then write "Here are some things I appreciate about you." Make enough copies of the sheet so that each student will have one.	prepared sheets of paper
AND			
The Next Step (key)	5 minutes	No preparation	student journals

Walk in the Light

get ready

Supplies: flashlights, plastic bags, night-lights or candles and matches

Teacher Tips: If flashlights aren't available, have the youth color a picture with crayons, build something out of small building blocks, or put together a simple jigsaw puzzle.

If it is impossible to make your room dark, ask the youth to close their eyes for this activity or put blindfolds on the youth. Or you might move the group to another room, such as a basement, that can easily be made dark.

jump in

Supplies: large sheets of paper, markers, tape

look for life

Supplies: Bibles

Without Light (5–8 minutes)

Allow the youth to talk about the dark atmosphere in the classroom while you wait for everyone to arrive. You can ask them to talk about whether they like the dark and to tell a story about something they did or like to do in the dark.

When everyone has arrived, extinguish the candles or turn off the night-lights. Have the youth form groups of two or three and have the groups line up on one side of the room. Stand up and say: "Somehow come to me and get a bag filled with something. Take it back to your area, and try to assemble it. Once you have it put together, test it to make sure that it works. But then stop using it until I call time."

While they are reassembling the flashlights (or putting together a substitute item), monitor for safety. After most groups are finished or frustrated, call time by lighting the candles or turning on the night-lights.

Ask:

- How many of you were able to get your flashlight (puzzle, Legos, and so forth) put together? Why, or why not?
- Could you have been more successful if you had been able to see better? Why?
- How important is light? What does light do for us?
- What does darkness do to us?

Talking about Light and Darkness (7–8 minutes)

Have each pair join with another pair. Pass out two sheets of large paper and markers to each group. Say: "Today we are going to be exploring what it means to walk in the light of Christ. 'Walking in the light' is a phrase that you might be unfamiliar with, so I'd like you to do some thinking about things you associate with the light and things you associate with darkness. Use one sheet of paper to come up with as many things as you can that relate to the light, and use the other to come up with as many things as you can that relate to darkness. You have about three minutes to work on your lists."

After about a minute and a half, tell them to start the other list if they've only been working on one of them. After three minutes, have each group tell about their lists. Tape them up on the wall, grouping the light and dark responses in separate areas.

A Faith Trial (10–15 minutes)

Ask:

- In a court of law, what is a testimony? (*A person's truthful recounting of a story*)

- What do you think it means to share your faith testimony? (*To tell your own story of faith to someone else*)

Say: "There's a story in the Bible where Jesus once gave his testimony in front of a group that was a little like a jury. Let's take a look at it."

Hand out Bibles and ask everyone to turn to John 8:12-20. Ask for volunteers to read the parts of the narrator, Jesus, and the Pharisees. Have them stand together at the front of the room. Say: "Let's try to act this out a bit and use this text as our script. Narrator, you're up first."

Have everyone read their parts, and then ask:

- Why did the Pharisees think that Jesus' testimony was not valid? (*Because their law required two witnesses, so someone else would have had to testify with Jesus.*)
- Whom did the Pharisees think Jesus expected to be his other witness? (*His earthly father.*)
- Why did Jesus say his testimony was indeed valid? (*Because his origin and his destiny resided with God.*)

Say: "We're going to create a little courtroom drama of our own. Some of you will be prosecutors or defense lawyers, some of you will testify, plus we'll need a judge and a jury." Depending on the size of your class, get volunteers for the roles of judge, prosecuting attorney, defense attorney, witness on behalf of the accused, and jury members.

Say: "Here's the story. [Name of the person on trial] is on trial for his or her faith. The question being asked is if there is enough evidence to convince the jury that he or she is indeed a follower of Jesus. You'll have a few minutes to prepare your case. The accused, the defense attorney, and the witness should work together on one team. The prosecuting attorney and the judge can work on another team. The jury should decide what they'd need to hear that would convince them of the real faith of the accused. You have three minutes to talk about your roles."

When about three minutes have passed or the groups have finished, conduct a mock trial. Let the youth have fun with their roles, but if things get too rowdy remind them that this is a courtroom. Be sure that the accused individual has the opportunity to testify to his or her faith, and that the witness gets a chance to verify the information. If you have time, feel free to switch roles (but don't take as long for the preparations the second time around.)

When the trial is over, say: "The question we need to each ask of ourselves is if people would really know that we are walking in the light. Can people see it in your actions, hear it in your words, and feel it when they are around you?" (Pause for the youth to consider this for a moment.)

Ask:

- One of the most common descriptions that John, the writer of the fourth gospel in the Bible, uses to describe Jesus is that he is the light. Why would John call Jesus a light?
- When has Jesus been a light to you?

Teacher Tip: Make this activity as complex or as simple as you like. For example, you could simply have a person testify, a friend corroborate his or her testimony, and a judge. Also, if you feel that you will not get a volunteer to be on trial for his or her faith, you can be the first volunteer.

An alternative is to have students do the last section of page 13 in the student journal.

Walk in the Light

Teacher Tip: If it has been a while since you have given your own testimony, you may want to do so here. Simply tell how Jesus has been the light in your life.

Teacher Tip: You may use page 14 in the student journal as an alternative means for this activity.

go with god

Supplies: prepared sheets of paper

Entitle a sheet of paper "I See Your Light." Leave space to write a name. Then write "Here are some things I appreciate about you." Make enough copies of the sheet so that each student will have one.

Supplies: student journals, pens or pencils

AND

Sharing Your Story (7–10 minutes)

Divide the youth into groups of three or four.

Say: "When you light a candle or flip on a light switch, everything is different because of the glow of the light. Likewise, one of the things it means to walk in the light is that the light that is in you shines on everyone you meet. That happens not only by people seeing your actions but also by your sharing how you are different because of knowing Jesus. Spend a few minutes telling one another about when you first learned about Jesus. Then talk about what you have been learning about him lately. Start with the person who is wearing the most colors and then go around the circle."

After a few minutes, call the groups back together.

I See Your Light (4–10 minutes)

Hand out copies of the prepared sheets of paper entitled "I See Your Light." Have everyone put his or her name on the top of the page.

Say: "In the next few minutes, I want you to think about the good qualities you see in one another. Then write down those good qualities on each person's sheet. Please take this seriously, and think about what will help the person better understand his or her good qualities. This is not a time for joking. You do not have to sign your name to the comments."

Give the youth time to move around the room and record their compliments. Be sure that you do this as well.

When everyone is done, let the youth silently read what others wrote on their paper.

Say: "Jesus wants us to walk in his light. Look over the list that your friends wrote for you. These are some of the ways that you already walk in the light. You don't want to become arrogant about this list, but it is OK to be pleased. Sometime today, spend a few moments thanking God for this list."

Then say: "Look at a person next to you and say to him or her: 'You are good! God has given you many good things!' "

AND

The Next Step (5 minutes)

Hand out the student journals, and play some soft music in the background. Give the youth about five minutes to complete pages 12–15 in their journals. Then end by singing together "This Little Light of Mine."

24

Walk the Talk

4

Walk in Darkness

Topic: Faithfulness and purity

Scripture: 1 John 1:5-2:1; 2:9-11

Key Verse: "If we say that we have fellowship with him while we are walking in darkness, we lie and do not do what is true" (1 John 1:6).

Take-Home Learning: Those who wish to walk the talk must not walk in darkness.

Younger Youth and the Topic

Movies like the *Lord of the Rings* trilogy and books such as the Harry Potter series are enormously popular with younger youth because they truly understand their world view. For most younger youth, life is filled with right and wrong, yes and no, truth and lies. They tend not to view the world as filled with shades of gray. They want a world where the light prevails, but they know that often the dark seems more powerful and appealing.

Younger Christian teenagers need to know three things:

1. God is greater than the darkness. Even when darkness seems to prevail, God is still the lord over darkness.

2. Calling oneself a Christian means making difficult choices along the way. In God there can be no darkness, so in our lives we cannot simply rationalize away certain behaviors. There are things we must simply choose not to do. Otherwise, darkness will continue to seem even more prominent in the world.

3. If they decide to walk in the light, they will not be alone. Even if their friends prefer to do things in the dark, there are many other teens and people around the world who are choosing to be bearers of light.

Theology and the Topic

At this time in history, we are living in a post-Christian era. One of the side effects of this is that moral, ethical, and religious instruction comes in many ways and from many places. Not all of this teaching is, of course, consistent with Christian doctrine. Thus, the situation of many youth today is one in which they are influenced by what the early church would have called "false teachers."

Walk in Darkness

Read all of **1 John.**

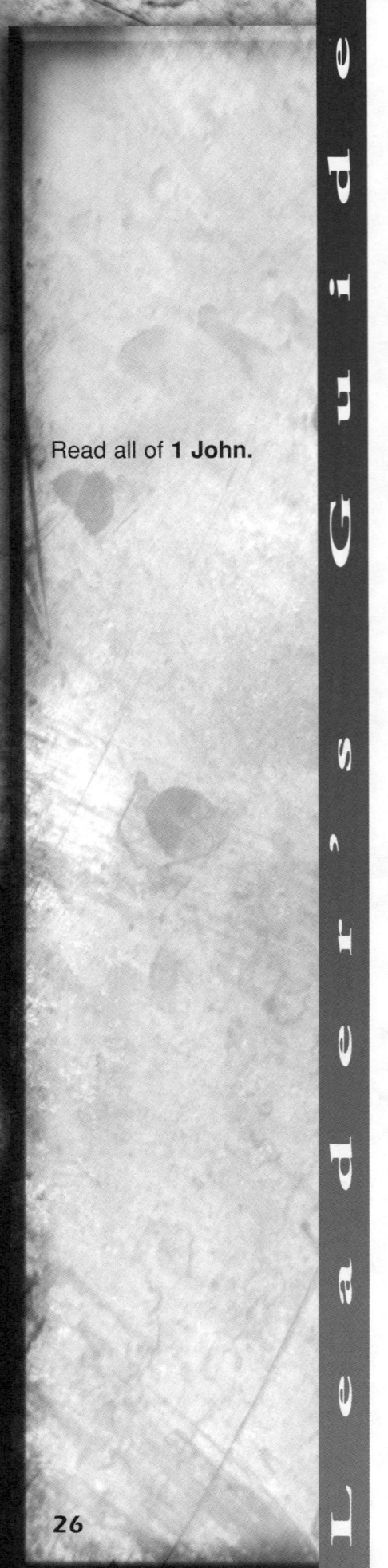

In such a time as this, what should we focus on in the Christian church when we are teaching our youth? How can we ensure that our faith continues to be passed on? One significant answer is the same one that was true for the early church during the time in which 1 John was written. We must help youth understand—and rehearse—the core doctrines of the faith.

For youth who hear many messages about God, it is important that we communicate clearly the theological understanding of God that undergirds 1 John. But 1 John also makes it clear that we must not just know about God. Faith, to be valid, must not simply be an intellectual endeavor but an experienced and lived reality. We learn about God most clearly by learning to love others.

You and the Scripture

The Book of 1 John is much beloved by Christians for its emphasis on love, its references to us as "little children," its simple clarity about what it means to be a follower of Christ, and its memorable passages. If you have a little extra time this week, read the entire letter several times—it's not at all long or difficult to read—and soak in its simple truths. At the very least, be sure to read carefully the first two chapters.

At the same time, many people have difficulty understanding just what the author was writing about at various points in the letter. Often when we read 1 John, we get the impression that we're jumping in on a conversation but are only hearing one person's speech. We have to read between the lines to uncover the other voice.

As you read 1 John, keep in mind that the author was asking this Johannine community (that is, a community which had likely been significantly influenced by the Gospel of John) to beware of false teachers in their midst. These misguided individuals had been members of the community at one time but had split off and had several significantly different teachings that did not conform to the church's doctrine, the beliefs held to be true by the community of faith over time.

Use this space to make notes about the evidence you find of what these false teachers were encouraging their followers to believe. You can also note some of the author's key arguments as you come across them. Finally, be sure to record any passages that especially strike home as you think about your own relationships with others.

Walk in Darkness

Scripture: 1 John 1:5-2:1; 2:9-11

Take-Home Learning: Those who wish to walk the talk must not walk in darkness.

🗝 indicates key activity. If time is limited, focus here.

activity	time	preparation	supplies

get ready

| 🗝 Incompatible | 10–12 minutes | No preparation | index cards, pens or pencils, paper clips, coin |

jump in

| Safety Tips | 3–5 minutes | No preparation | large sheets of paper, markers, tape |

look for life

| 🗝 If-Then | 6–9 minutes | No preparation | Bibles, large sheets of paper, markers, tape |

AND

| 🗝 100 Percent Pure | 2–4 minutes | No preparation | bar of Ivory® soap, bottled water |

go with god

| The Next Step | 5–7 minutes | No preparation | student journals, pens or pencils |

OR

| Fizzled Away | 2–4 minutes | Put water into the large, clear glass bowl and tablets in small bowls. Put the bowls on tables around which the students will sit. | small bowls; large, clear glass bowl; water; effervescent denture tablets; pencils or fine-point markers |

Walk in Darkness

get ready

Supplies: index cards, pens or pencils, paper clips, coin

Leader's Guide

Incompatible (10–12 minutes)

As the youth arrive, assign them to one of two groups. The first should secretly write on index cards pairs of things that are (generally) incompatible with one another. For example:

- Guppies & Piranhas
- Alcohol & prescription drugs
- Chevy & Ford car parts
- Salt water & thirst

The second group should secretly write on index cards pairs of things that are (generally) compatible with one another. For example:

- Coffee & creamer
- AA batteries & personal CD players
- Bees & flowers
- Screws & nuts
- Blue jeans & t-shirts

Each item should be written clearly on a separate index card, with the pairs of items kept or paper clipped together. Each group should pick the five pairings they think are the best. If they need ideas, share some of the ones above with them.

Flip a coin to see which group starts first. Have them choose two players to be the ones who will pantomime the paired items from the other team's cards. Say: "You will have 45 seconds to pantomime one of the items that the other team came up with. The other players on your team have to correctly identify both items. You should both pantomime your items at the same time. Are you ready? Go!"

Ask someone on the opposing team to keep time. If both items are guessed within 45 seconds, give the team a point. Then let the other team have a turn. Continue alternating teams until you have gone through all the pairs from each team. The team with the most points wins.

Say: "Here's one more pair for you to think about. Tell me if these two are compatible or incompatible. God, and darkness." *(incompatible)*

Safety Tips (3–5 minutes)

Ask the following questions and write the students' answers on large paper:

- What are some of the common safety tips or rules that apply to dark places or to the night? *(Don't go out alone, leave a light on at home if you'll be gone, be home by a certain hour.)*
- Why do rules and guidelines like these exist? *(For safety and security)*
- What are some things that are more likely to happen in the darkness than in the light? *(crimes, vandalism, sneaking around)*
- Why do these things happen more often in the dark? *(Because people have something to hide; no one will know what they are doing.)*
- Why do we say that the things we do which we wouldn't want others to know about come from our "dark side"?

jump in

Supplies: large sheets of paper, markers, tape

Walk the Talk

If-Then (6–9 minutes)

Hand out Bibles, large paper, and markers. Say: "Today we're going to be looking at a part of the letter of 1 John. The author of this letter was warning a group of faithful Christians about the errors of a group of Christians who had split from the community. In other words, it would be as if a former pastor of this church wrote us a letter to warn us about some things that some ex-church members were teaching."

Divide the youth into groups of two to four people. Say: "In your groups, read 1 John 1:5–2:1. Then, in your own words, see if you can figure out which are the three errors John was opposed to and which are the three truths he wanted his faithful believers to know. In each case, rewrite it as an 'if-then' statement."

Answers:

Errors

If we say that we're friends with God but walk in darkness, then we're not doing what we should and are being deceitful.

If we say that we are without sin in our lives, we're wrong and don't know the truth.

If we say that we haven't sinned, we've made a liar out of Jesus.

Truths

If we walk in the light, then we live in unity with one another and are forgiven.

If we confess our sin, then we will be forgiven.

If we have sinned, then Jesus will be our advocate with God.

Give the youth about four to five minutes to work, then ask for volunteers to state the three errors and the three truths.

Ask:

- What does John mean by the phrase "walking in darkness"? (*Sin; not living in unity with our brothers and sisters; not living lives of love*)
- What are the two things we need to do to be sure we're not walking in darkness? (*Walk in the light* [*that is, love others*] *and recognize and confess our sin.*)

AND

100 Percent Pure (2–4 minutes)

Hold up a bar of Ivory® soap in its package. Read the line about how it is "99 44/100% pure®."

---

look for life

Supplies: Bibles, large sheets of paper, markers, tape

Teacher Tip: Consider adding a few minutes to this activity for youth to do page 16 in the student journal.

Supplies: bar of Ivory® soap, bottled water

Walk in Darkness

Ask:

- What does it mean to say that this bar of soap is 99 44/100% pure®? Is it completely pure?

Hold up a commercial bottle of water (which has trace amounts of salt, minerals, and so on added to it.)

Ask:

- If you buy a bottle of water, what do you expect to be in it?

Read the list of ingredients. Ask:

- Would you consider this to be pure water? Why, or why not?

Read 1 John 1:5. Ask:

- If God is 100 percent pure, with no darkness at all, what do you think the people of God are to be like? (*Pure, without sin*)
- Does that mean that believers will never sin or walk in darkness? (*No*)
- If we know that we are to be pure but also know that we aren't, what are we to do? (*Confess our sins and receive God's cleansing grace which comes through Jesus*)

The Next Step (5–7 minutes)

Hand out the student journals. Play some soft music in the background while the youth reflect in their journals, pages 16–19. Give the students about five minutes to work, then collect the journals.

OR

Fizzled Away (2–4 minutes)

Place bowls of effervescent denture tablets on the tables, and hand out pencils or fine-point markers. Have another large, clear glass bowl or pitcher filled most of the way with water.

Say: "I'd like you to think for a few moments in silence about the ways in which you are walking in darkness. In other words, what things do you do that are sinful, that you are not proud of, or that keep you from being pure. Then take one of the tablets and write on it a word or phrase that describes that behavior or attitude. You may write more than one thing on each tablet, or you can use more than one tablet if you'd like to. When you have the words written on your tablets, take a moment to pray that you would experience and accept God's forgiveness. When you're ready, bring your tablet up to the glass bowl and drop it in."

When everyone is finished, say: "Just as the water dissolves the tablets, God can melt away those parts of our lives which we'd like to hide and which we know are wrong. Now go forth as forgiven people, who walk in the light of God and not in the darkness of the world."

---

go with god

Supplies: student journals, pens or pencils

Supplies: small bowls; large, clear glass bowl; water; effervescent denture tablets; pencils or fine-point markers

Walk the Talk

5

Walk to Emmaus

Topic: Walking with others on our journey

Scripture: Luke 24:13-35

Key Verse: They said to each other, "Were not our hearts burning within us while he was talking to us on the road, while he was opening the Scriptures to us?" (Luke 24:32).

Take-Home Learning: Walking the road of faith is often better when we have people who will walk with us—especially during the darkest times of our lives.

Younger Youth and the Topic

During the late pre-adolescent and early teen years, youth begin to separate themselves from their families. They start spending a majority of their free time with friends and other peers who become a "second family" to them. Parents sometimes wonder during this time of life what has happened to their children, for it often seems like they no longer have the influence over their kids that they once did. The peer group becomes a primary place where youth can test new behaviors, beliefs, and styles as they form and shape their identity.

This separating is completely normal, but teens still need and desire the regular presence of adults in their lives. They often are especially open to the ideas and stories of adults other than their parents during this time in their life. Adults can offer perspective and experience—two things peers generally cannot. Especially during the difficult moments of their lives, younger teens need a loving adult who will walk with them on their journey. When others experience crisis in their lives, people of faith have a great opportunity to express love.

This session will give your class members some great adult attention. During the class, the youth will have the opportunity to hear some faith and personal stories from a few adults from your congregation. Often we think of mentoring as a long, time-intensive process. While that assessment can be true, mentoring can also occur during a short one-time event. What you want to accomplish should determine the mentoring style that is used.

Ideally, you should try to recruit one mentor for every two youth in your class. Who can be mentors? Senior citizens from your church, the pastor and other church leaders, mature college students, business people with

Check with a pastor for recommendations of people who would be a great mentor or faith-related storyteller.

Walk to Emmaus

31

Read **Luke 24:13-35** as a story of mentoring.

Session Preparation

Before this session, you will need to invite some mentors to your class. Depending on the ratio of youth to mentors, arrange chairs in groups. For instance, if you have a 2 to 1 ratio, you will want to put three chairs to a group. There should be a group of chairs for each mentor.

the same interests as your youth, parents with a deep faith—the list of possible mentors is endless, but the goal is to offer as much diversity as possible. Write down the names of people who come to mind as you read the above list.

Call and personally invite the people you choose to come to your class. Be sure to explain the purpose of the class, the class time and date, where you meet, and what you wish to have them share. Encourage them to think of a story they could share about a time when their faith sustained them through a crisis.

As you are recruiting your mentors, reassure them that they do not have to have all the right answers. Their main job is to share their personal story, to give the youth attention, and to begin to build some adult-youth friendships that may extend beyond the class.

Theology and the Topic

Emptiness. Loneliness. Despair. In the midst of our darkest hour, Christ comes to us, comforting and sustaining us until we find a way through our pain. What was central in the Emmaus story (Luke 24:13-35) is the presence of Christ during a dark time. In essence, this was the church's encounter with the living Christ. Likewise, the people with whom we choose to walk on our journey can embody Christ for us. Thus, as adults who are mature in faith, our own walk with Christ empowers us to embody Christ for the youth whom we know.

You and the Scripture

Jesus came on the road and walked *with* the two disciples. He came to be with others, just as he had throughout his ministry. There are some practical steps outlined in this story that can help us learn to mentor others:

Luke 24:15—Jesus came to the men on the road. He approached them. In this case, his approach came after a major crisis in their lives.

Luke 24:17-18—Jesus began by asking a simple question of them. However, this question really hit them right where they were at that time.

Luke 24:19-24—Jesus let them do the talking. He waited patiently and listened carefully. In essence, Jesus was letting them make room for what he had to say.

Luke 24:25-27—Jesus, the mentor, taught them.

Luke 24:28—Jesus did not overstay his welcome. Apparently, Jesus was ready to end his time with them before they were ready to end their time with Jesus. This technique is a good to use with teens; it keeps them motivated to continue the relationship.

Luke 24:34—Here is the ultimate goal in our mentoring relationships with youth. Like the disciples, we want our youth to proclaim, "The Lord has really risen!"

Walk to Emmaus

Scripture: Luke 24:13-35

Take-Home Learning: Walking the road of faith is often better when we have people who will walk with us—especially during the darkest times of our lives.

indicates key activity. If time is limited, focus here.

activity	time	preparation	supplies
get ready			
Walking the Emmaus Road	7–10 minutes	Arrange chairs in groups of three	Bibles, chairs
jump in			
Preparing for Our Walk	6–10 minutes	No preparation	large sheets of paper, markers, tape, nametags
OR			
Introductions and Preparations	8–12 minutes	Photocopy "What I Am Hearing" (page 50).	ball, copies of "What I Am Hearing" (page 50), pens
OR			
Starting	3–5 minutes	No preparation	None
look for life			
Walking the Road	5–12 minutes	No preparation	None
AND			
The Deepest Part	8–15 minutes	Photocopy "What I Am Hearing" (page 50).	copies of "What I Am Hearing" (page 50), pens
go with god			
In the Breaking of the Bread	5–7 minutes	Invite your pastor to end the class with a Communion service.	Communion items
OR			
Ending the Journey	5–7 minutes	No preparation	paper or simple pre-printed thank-you notes, pens, markers
OR			
The Next Step	5–7 minutes	No preparation	student journals, pens or pencils

Walk to Emmaus

get ready

Supplies: Bibles, chairs

Walking the Emmaus Road (7–10 minutes)

As youth arrive, ask them to sit in the arranged chairs but not to move them. Encourage them to talk to the others in their group about favorite vacations—where they went, how they got there, with whom they went.

Say: "After Jesus' death, the disciples were depressed, confused, and afraid. Their teacher and friend had just been brutally executed, and they were not sure what to do next. That's when something happened that changed their lives forever." Direct the students to take turns reading Luke 24:13-35 aloud in their small groups.

When everyone is done, ask:

- What two things enabled the disciples to recognize Christ? (*Jesus' interpretation of the Hebrew Scriptures and the breaking of the bread*)
- Why do we all sometimes need people to help us to understand and apply Scripture?
- How do we experience Jesus during Communion, the breaking of the bread?
- How did this time with Jesus affect the two people?
- If you were able to walk with Jesus, what would you want to talk about?

Preparing for Our Walk (6–10 minutes)

Say: "Today I have invited a number of people to come to our class. (Briefly tell them who is coming and a little about each person). Each of you will have a chance to talk to as many of these people as possible. You can ask them questions, and you can tell them things about yourself. They will also share some stories with you about their faith. My hope is this will be our Emmaus Road. Be sure to listen for their secrets to living a meaningful life. Look for the way they do things and how that could help you in your life."

Say: "In the next few minutes, I want your group to come up with some questions to ask these people. You might ask simple questions such as, 'Did you graduate from high school?' or more complicated questions such as, 'What made you choose your career?' Be sure to ask two or three questions about their experience of faith. Write the questions on large paper. When you fill up the paper, hang it up on the wall. You can fill up two or three sheets if you want to. Also, write your name on a nametag and put it on."

OR

Introductions and Preparations (8–12 minutes)

Have the youth and mentors stand in a circle. On your count of three they are to pass the ball around the circle as quickly as possible. Count quickly before they can talk or plan a strategy. Time them.

Say: "That was pretty quick, but not a world record. I think that you can do that quicker. But before we try again, let's introduce ourselves. I'd like

jump in

Supplies: large sheets of paper, markers, tape, nametags

Teacher Tips: Help each group get started. Be prepared to give sample questions. Encourage the groups to look at the other groups' questions.

If time is short, make up a list of suggested questions, but give the youth a few minutes to add their own questions.

While students work, keep an eye out for the mentors as they arrive. Greet them and thank them. Give each a nametag and marker. Encourage them to read the questions on the large papers.

Walk the Talk

the youth to tell us your name and describe what you think you will be like as an adult. If you are not sure, then make a guess. Mentors, tell us your name and describe what you were like when you were about the same age as these youth. If you don't remember, you may guess too."

Give the ball to the first person to start. When finished, he or she passes the ball to the next person until it has gone around the room.

Say: "Welcome everyone. Now, getting back to our world record...how could this team get the ball around the room more quickly?" Let them come up with strategies and try again to beat their score. When they beat their first time, say: "When we work together, we can do great things!"

Then invite each mentor to sit down in a separate grouping of chairs. Invite the youth to take a seat in one of the remaining chairs. Pass out the reproducible page and pens to the youth.

Say: "You will notice several sections in your reproducible page. One section is called What I Am Hearing—it is to be used to keep track of what the mentors are saying. You may record direct quotes and/or just general ideas. Another section is called More Questions. If you think of other good questions you want to ask one of the adults, write them down. The third section is I'm Learning. Use this section to record any your learnings. The section called The Rubber Meets the Road is for writing about how you will use the things you are learning. But, you don't have to fill it out now, unless you want to."

OR

Starting (3–5 minutes)

Say: "To get you started, talk about the answers to these questions:

- What was your family like when you were growing up?
- What was the most difficult thing you have ever gone through?

" Once those questions are answered, start asking other questions. By the way, youth, you also need to answer the questions. Mentors, you may ask you questions as well."

Keep this first round short.

Walking the Road (5–12 minutes)

Ask the youth to switch to a different mentor. The youth do not need to stay with the same youth unless they want to, but keep the group size consistent throughout.

Walk around to the groups, and make sure that the youth are participating and listening. Encourage any youth who are struggling to come up with questions to ask some from the large sheets of paper throughout the room.

Walk to Emmaus

Leader's Guide

Supplies: ball, copies of "What I Am Hearing" (page 50), pens

If class time is less than 45 minutes, or if your class or church is very small, you can skip this activity and simply introduce yourselves.

Teacher Tip: If you are unable to get mentors to come for this session, use the material in the student journal (pages 20–23) to prompt discussion.

look for life

Supplies: copies of "What I Am Hearing" (page 50), pens

The amount of time needed for this activity depends on the ratio of your group. The higher the ratio, the more time you will need.

go with god

Supplies: Communion items

Supplies: paper or simple pre-printed thank-you notes, pens, markers

Teacher Tip: Write the names of the mentors on a large sheet of paper so that the youth can see how to spell them correctly. Be prepared to offer some ideas of what the youth can write.

Supplies: student journals, pens or pencils

After 5–10 minutes, call time. Ask for volunteers to tell about something they learned. Give a few minutes for sharing. Then have the youth switch to a different mentor and repeat the process.

AND

The Deepest Part (8–15 minutes)

This is the last round of dialogues. When the youth have switched, ask the mentors to talk specifically this time about their spiritual life. The mentors can share their testimony, especially a story of how their faith supported them in a time of difficulty. Allow time for questions.

Encourage the youth to write on the section of the reproducible page entitled "The Spiritual Side." Thank the mentors again for their participation and tell them they are free to leave at this time (unless you are planning to do the Communion activity below).

In the Breaking of the Bread (6–10 minutes)

End together with Communion. Tell the pastor that you are studying the Emmaus story and ask her or him to incorporate the story into the liturgy.

OR

Ending the Journey (5–7 minutes)

Invite the youth to write or draw thank-you notes to the mentors. They may want to write individual notes to one or two of the mentors or write a sentence or two on a group note. If the students are writing individual notes, remind them that their notes from the conversations are a good source for telling the mentors what was especially meaningful to them. Collect the thank-you notes and place them in large envelopes for mailing.

OR

The Next Step (5–7 minutes)

Hand out the student journals and pens or pencils. Play some quiet music in the background and give the youth about five minutes to do pages 20–23 in the student journal.

Collect the journals, and close with a short prayer of thanks for the gift of friends who join us on our journey and represent the presence of Christ during the dark times of life.

Walk as He Walked

Topic: The ways Jesus lived his faith

Scripture: 1 John 2:3-6; Matthew 8:1-4; 9:10-13, 35-38; 12:1-8; 18:1-5, 21-35; Mark 10:17-27; Luke 4:42-44; 5:15-16; 22:24-27

Key Scripture: "Whoever says, 'I abide in him,' ought to walk just as he walked" (1 John 2:6).

Take-Home Learning: As followers of Jesus, we are to imitate his life.

Younger Youth and the Topic

If you sit in a shopping mall and people-watch for a while, you'll quickly notice that teens often imitate one another. Although they may have individual preferences and styles, a teen will imitate much about his or her friends—clothing, values, musical tastes, dance moves, and so on. One reason younger youth, especially, imitate one another is so they don't stand out too much from the crowd. Teenagers generally don't like to be singled out as different.

Younger youth are searching for role models to pattern their lives after. What better model can we offer them than Jesus? Yet while many youth would label themselves Christians, far fewer would say that they are consciously trying to imitate Jesus. Some are afraid of being seen as too religious, while others often find it difficult to understand how one could possibly imitate someone whom they see as perfect.

Help the youth to discover that there are many ways to imitate the love and compassion of Jesus without being preachy about their faith. In addition, encourage them to be supportive of one another and to covenant with other Christian friends as they strive to walk like Jesus. Faith should never be understood to be a solitary endeavor.

Theology the Topic

One of the most difficult theological issues for Christian scholars is to explain just how Jesus brings us salvation. The traditional answer espoused by many early theologians as well as Martin Luther is that Jesus' death paid the price of our sin once and for all as a ransom so that we would no longer be enslaved to evil. But that assertion is certainly not the only theological or biblical understanding of what salvation means.

The "moral influence theory," originated by Abelard (A.D. 1079–1142), explains that Jesus Christ's sacrificial love on the cross motivates us to

Check with your pastor for recommendations of people who would be a great mentor or faith-related storyteller.

Walk as He Walked

Read **1 John, especially 2:3-8; 3:22-24; 4:21; and 5:2-3.**

respond to God's love rather than to guilt or fear. In this tradition, a later influential Christian educator, Horace Bushnell (1802–1881), saw love as a greater power than punishment and the whole life of Jesus, not just his death, as a redemptive act.

Our purpose here is not to come to a conclusion for one position over the other. However, when we believe that we are called to walk as Jesus walked, we find we have to look closely at the way he lived his life so that we might be more like him in our every action.

To walk as Jesus walked means knowing with whom he chose to be and why. It means understanding his concept of the Kingdom of God and how that shaped his storytelling and his life. It means being willing to go wherever we believe God calls us to go, even if it leads us to the cross.

You and the Scripture

In preparation for this week's lesson, take time to read most or all of the stories on the reproducible page. After reading each one, meditate on it for a time. Ask yourself these questions:

- What would the people in this story have found exciting, inviting, and igniting about Jesus?
- What does this story say to me about the kind of life Jesus lived?
- In what ways am I like or unlike the Jesus in this story? How could I be more like him?

When the writer of 1 John talks about obeying Jesus' commandments, he is especially referring to the commandment to love your neighbor as yourself. This focus becomes especially clear later in the letter, particularly in 2:7-8, 3:22-24, 4:21, and 5:2-3. Thus abiding in Jesus is not simply a matter of spiritual communion, of feeling one with Jesus. Abiding in Jesus must always be paired with intentionally loving acts. How have you been abiding lately?

Walk the Talk

Walk as He Walked

Scripture: 1 John 2:3-6; Matthew 8:1-4; 9:10-13, 35-38; 12:1-8; 18:1-5, 21-35; Mark 10:17-27; Luke 4:42-44; 5:15-16; 22:24-27

Take-Home Learning: As followers of Jesus, we are to imitate his life.

indicates key activity. If time is limited, focus here.

activity	time	preparation	supplies
get ready			
Make Some Feet	4–8 minutes	No preparation	Supplies: construction paper, pencils, scissors
AND			
Walk This Way	3–7 minutes	No preparation	None
jump in			
How Do You Know?	4–9 minutes	No preparation	Bibles
AND			
Jesus Through the Magnifying Glass	5–8 minutes	Make two or three copies of pages 53–54 and cut out the magnifying glasses on them.	Bibles, pens, magnifying glass (optional), magnifying glass cutouts (pages 53–54), feet cutouts from the first activity
look for life			
In His Steps	6–10 minutes	No preparation	footprints from the first activity
go with god			
A True Story	2–4 minutes	No preparation	None
OR			
The Next Step	2–4 minutes	No preparation	student journals, pens or pencils, footprints made earlier

Walk as He Walked

get ready

Supplies: construction paper, pencils, scissors

Leader's Guide

Make Some Feet (4–8 minutes)

As the youth arrive, ask them to take their shoes and socks off and trace one of their feet onto a piece of construction paper. Provide scissors for them to cut the feet out. Each person should make at least two feet.

While they work, ask them to share childhood memories of Sunday school. If they didn't go as children, ask what brought them to church later on.

AND

Walk This Way (3–7 minutes)

Ask:

- How many of you have ever played Follow the Leader? What makes that game fun?

Say: "We're going to play our own version of the game, but we'll call it Walk This Way." Have everyone stand in two lines across from a partner.

Then say: "Each of you needs to think up some unusual way to walk across a room. You'll demonstrate it for all of us, and then your partner has to try to imitate your walk as closely as possible. When it's your turn, go to the opposite end of the room and walk back to your place in line. We'll start with the first person in this line." (*Choose one of the two lines.*)

When everyone in one line has had a turn making up a walk, let the other team's members lead the walks. Keep the atmosphere light-hearted so that everyone gets a good laugh out of the activity. After everyone has had a chance to imitate someone (there's no need to keep track of who does the best job, by the way), ask everyone to sit down.

Ask:

- Would it ever possible to imitate someone exactly? Why, or why not?" (*Probably not, although you might get pretty close with practice.*)

Say: "Today we're exploring what it means to walk as Jesus walked. Just as we had to watch our partners closely to be able to imitate them, we have to look closely at Jesus' life to be able to imitate him."

How Do You Know? (4–9 minutes)

Say: "With your partner, think of a question that starts with the words, 'How do you know . . . ?' For example, your question might be, 'How do you know when spaghetti pasta is cooked just right?' You must know the answer to your question. See whether you can think of a question that will stump the rest of us. You'll have 72 seconds to come up with a question."

Give the youth 72 seconds to work, then ask each pair to relate their question. Let a volunteer guess the answer. End by asking: "How do you know when a person really knows Jesus?" Take a few answers, then hand out the Bibles. Together read 1 John 2:3-6.

jump in

Supplies: Bibles

If class time is short, make a list of questions and answers to hand out. Give the youth a couple of minutes to add a question or two of their own.

Walk the Talk

Ask:

- After reading this, how would you answer the question, How do you know when a person really knows Jesus? (*If he or she obeys Jesus' commandments.*)
- Which commandments do you think the author of the letter meant? (*He particularly is referring to the commandment to love. See 1 John 2:7-8, 3:22-24; John 13:34.*)
- What does it mean to "abide in him" (verse 6)? (*To dwell or remain in God, to be intimate with God.*)
- So what must we do if we say we're intimate with God? (*Walk as Jesus walked by loving others.*)

AND

Jesus Through the Magnifying Glass (5–8 minutes)

Divide the youth into small groups. Hand out Bibles and pens. If you have a real magnifying glass, hold it up.

Say: "Magnifying glasses help us examine things more closely. You're each going to be getting a story or two from Jesus' life that tells us something about what he was like. In each case, the story will have a question with it that will help you to examine more deeply what was happening in the story. See if you can figure out what people thought was so surprising or amazing about Jesus' actions. Then write in large letters on one of the feet cutouts a word or phrase that represents what you found out about Jesus."

Distribute the magnifying glass questions and the feet to each group. Make sure that you have two or three stories and feet to give to each group. Give the youth about four minutes to read and answer the stories they were assigned.

After everyone has finished, have the groups share what they've written on their foot cutouts. Then ask: "These are just some of the stories that tell us about the kind of life Jesus lived and encouraged others to follow. Can you think of other qualities of his life that we should imitate to walk as he walked?" If others are suggested, write them down on one of the cutouts.

In His Steps (6–10 minutes)

Lay the footprints out in a large circle around the room, moving furniture out of the way as necessary. Invite everyone to stand by one of them.

Say: "I'm going to read a scenario. I'd like you to think about the word or phrase on your footprint and think about how you could deal with that situation in the way that Jesus might. If you think it applies, then tell us how you might deal with the situation. More than one of you can answer if you think what is written on your footprint applies." Between each scenario, everyone should move one footprint to your right."

Walk as He Walked

Supplies: Bibles, pens, magnifying glass (optional), magnifying glass cutouts (pages 53–54), feet cutouts from the first activity

Before class, make two or three copies of pages 53–54 and cut out the magnifying glasses on them.

look for life

Supplies: footprints from the first activity

go with god

This true story is based on a a story from *Households of God on China's Soil,* compiled and translated by Raymond Fung (World Council of Churches, 1982), pages 52–53.

Supplies: student journals, pens or pencils, footprints made earlier

A True Story (2–4 minutes)

Read this story to the group, or have one of the youth read it to the class. Explain beforehand that coke is a hard, gray fuel made from coal.

In the not-too-distant past of the 1970's, far away in China there was a small rural village made up of two different ethnic groups Koreans and Han Chinese. Only a few of the villagers were Christian.

Trouble came with the winter. To heat their homes the people burned a fuel called coke. However, the Koreans felt that the Han Chinese were getting bigger and better coke pieces. Tensions rose between the two groups. Winter turned bitter, and a Korean baby died in the night when the family's fire burned out. His family was distraught and charged that that the poor quality coke was at fault.

Representatives from both sides gathered to work out a solution. Although there were Christians on both sides, the leaders made no progress. Then Brother Lee, whose wife was Han, offered to share his coke. No one thought much of the proposal. But day after day he took a few pounds of coke and gave it to a Korean family. Sometimes the Korean families were unreceptive to his friendly words, although they accepted the coke. But sometimes a family would not only accept the coke, but also offer him a cup of tea and visit for few moments.

One Sunday the Brother Lee's pastor told the congregation what he had been doing. He said, "Brother Lee has shown us the way; he alone acted like our Lord." When the family heads a few days later met again over the matter, Christians on both sides offered to share their coke, not only once, but on an ongoing basis. The deadlock was broken.

Within a year the whole village had become Christian. The people knew that Brother Lee and the other Christians were Jesus' disciples. They had demonstrated their love in sharing what they had. By walking as Jesus walked, their actions moved others to accept Christ as their Lord as well.

Ask:

- In what way was Brother Lee walking as Christ walked?
- What belief do you think was behind his actions?

OR

The Next Step (5–7 minutes)

Hand out the student journals and pens. Ask the youth to spread out around the room. Play some soft music in the background while they answer the questions. Give them about five minutes to work on page 24–27, then call them back together and collect the journals.

Join in a circle, standing on the footprints you made earlier. Join hands and pray that God would help you to walk as Jesus walked in all of the situations of life.

Walk the Talk

Walk in Newness of Life

Topic: Experiencing a changed life

Scripture: Romans 6:1-13; Philippians 1:6

Key Scripture: "Therefore we have been buried with him by baptism into death, so that, just as Christ was raised from the dead by the glory of the Father, so we too might walk in newness of life" (Romans 6:4).

Take-Home Learning: Trusting in Christ means that we no longer need to be bound by sin but can, instead, experience a new kind of life.

Younger Youth and the Topic

Younger youth experience something new practically every day. They wake up, look in the mirror, and feel—often rightly so—that they just don't have the same body they had the day before. Their friendships are continuously going through revisions, their interests change rapidly, and they experiment with new looks and new fads.

Yet at the same time, many young people are looking for a clean break from their past or a fresh start but don't know how to bring about this change. They may struggle with guilt about past actions or difficulty in overcoming bad habits and behaviors.

Younger youth desperately need to hear that we can be new creatures. They are not fated to be the way they are now. This concept is especially important for youth who are stuck in addictive behavior or other unhealthy habits. Many times youth feel absolutely helpless and hopeless in their ability to change. This session can infuse them with a sense of hope!

Theology and the Topic

An important question for Christians to continually ask themselves is this: "In what way am I different because I know Christ?" If our life isn't fundamentally changed by our relationship with Christ, of what use is that relationship? If we have indeed died to sin and trust God's saving grace, why do we continue living like everyone else? A life of sin is truly a contradiction to the kind of life we can have when we accept God's new life, which comes through Christ.

If we wish to experience new life in Christ, an important step toward that change is repentance. Youth can have a fresh start, but they also need to

Walk in Newness of Life

Read **Romans 6:1-7 and 6:8-13.**

After you read each Scripture, read the hints on the reproducible page for this session to help you further understand the passage.

repent—admitting what is wrong, accepting the consequences that follow, and turning in a new direction. Some youth will want the clean break from their old way of living without accepting the responsibility for or consequences of their actions.

Help the youth understand that the newness that God offers does not come about until we have put ourselves in the right position—one of repentance. Remind them of the promise of I John 1:9, "If we confess our sins, he who is faithful and just will forgive us our sins and cleanse us from all unrighteousness." God's grace is always working in our life—before we're even aware of it and through our entire lives—and God's forgiveness is unconditional.

You and the Scripture

Read Romans 6:1-7.

- How would you describe your life before you knew or made a serious commitment to Jesus?
- How would you describe the new life you now experience to a friend who didn't know Jesus?
- In what ways do you still feel enslaved by sin?
- In what ways do you feel freed from sin?

Read Romans 6:8-13.

- What sin do you still allow to have control over your life?
- What needs to happen for you to present your life and your body as an "instrument of righteousness" to God?

Walk the Talk

Walk in Newness of Life

Scripture: Romans 6:1-13; Philippians 1:6

Take-Home Learning: Trusting in Christ means that we no longer need to be bound by sin but can, instead, experience a new kind of life.

indicates key activity. If time is limited, focus here.

activity	time	preparation	supplies
get ready			
Where Is It?	5–15 minutes	Write out invitations to a different location where you will have your meeting. See details in the activity on page 45.	copies of the invitation for each participant, large sheets of paper, markers, tape
jump in			
Out With the Old 🔑	6–12 minutes	Have everyone bring a toy they no longer play with, a clothing item they've outgrown, or a book they loved as a child.	items brought by each participant
look for life			
When Is New Good? 🔑	8–15 minutes	No preparation	None
AND			
Tough Stuff Made Simple 🔑	8–12 minutes	Make photocopies of "Bible Tips," page 54, and cut the tips apart along the dotted lines.	copies of page 54 cut apart, several copies of several versions of the Bible, paper, pens
AND			
Perfected Blunders	6–8 minutes	Put a large container of sand in the corner of the room.	large container, smaller container, sand, student journals, pens or pencils
go with god			
The Next Step	5–9 minutes	No preparation	student journals, pens or pencils

Walk in Newness of Life

get ready

Supplies: copies of the invitation for each participant, large sheets of paper, markers, tape

The duration of this activity depends on the location. The more roundabout the directions can be, the better. However, be sure to watch the time. Additionally, off-site travel will probably require permission forms to be signed by a parent. If you choose to go elsewhere, contact the parents ahead.

If you typically have a lot of latecomers to your class and you'll be driving somewhere, be sure to have an extra adult who can bring late arrivals.

jump in

Supplies: items brought by each participant

A week before class, ask the class members to bring a toy they no longer play with, a clothing item they've outgrown, or a book they loved as a child. Give the youth a reminder call the night before class. Bring an item or two of your own.

Where Is It? (5–15 minutes)

If possible, plan on meeting in a different location from the room where you normally meet. A new house or building would be ideal—even if the structure is not completely finished. If this is not possible, make arrangements to swap rooms with another class. Design an invitation to the new location, with explicit directions; and post a copy on the door for each person. You should not be present when the youth arrive, although another adult should check to see that the youth are going where they should.

If your "new" location requires travel via vehicles, then wait for the youth in the parking lot and leave directions as to where to find you.

Post a large sheet of paper on the wall on which you've written the following questions with room to write around the questions:

- What do you see that is different from our usual location?
- What do you hear that's different?
- What do you smell?
- What do you feel?
- How does "new" feel?
- What words would you use to describe our old room?
- What "new" things do you look forward to the most? (*examples: new foods, new movies, new clothes, new classes*)
- How do you generally deal with new things and changes?

Give the youth time to get to the location. As the youth arrive, pair them up and have them answer the questions on the page you posted.

After they have answered, have the youth form small groups of three or four, and ask them to answer these questions:

- Do you like change? Why, or why not?
- What is the hardest thing about change?
- What is the easiest thing about change?
- What is the biggest thing in your life you have changed?

Out With the Old (6–12 minutes)

If your class has more than eight youth, split the youth into two groups. Have the youth tell about their item and the memories associated with it.

After everyone has had a chance to speak, ask:

- Why do our feelings about our possessions change over time?
- Can you think of something that is no longer important to you that was just a year or two ago?
- What would you think of a friend of yours who suddenly and consistently started acting five or ten years younger than he or she really was?

Say: "One thing that I've learned is that I'm constantly changing and growing. As I get older, some things that were once important to me no longer are. But also as I get older, new things or new people take on a

Walk the Talk

new importance. And that's a good thing, because we are supposed to outgrow our childish ways."

When Is New Good? (8–15 minutes)

Have the youth form pairs. Then say: "With your partner, come up with a story about a person who refused to grow up. Your story could be real, like a teenager who never learned to accept responsibility. Or it could be silly, like a bank executive who still has to hold his mommy's hand even in important meetings. Your team can tell the story or act it out."

Give the youth few minutes to come up with their idea, then have each pair or group present their story.

Ask:

- What happens to people when they don't change? (*They can't maintain relationships with friends; they are not happy; they get frustrated by the change happening around them.*)
- What do you think of persons who tell you that they have made a radical change to their life but they don't show it in their actions?

Say: "All of this talk today about old and new things has to do with our faith. When we decide to follow Christ and call ourselves Christian, we're new people. Just as it would be ridiculous to keep wearing children's clothes at your age, some things are ridiculous for us to keep doing."

AND

Tough Stuff Made Simple (8–12 minutes)

Hand out Bibles and have everyone turn to Romans 6. Say: "Romans 6 is a really tough chapter to understand. So we're going to do some looking at different translations of the Bible to help us make sense of it."

Divide the youth into groups of two or three, and give each group as many different translations as you can find, especially more contemporary ones like the NRSV, NIV, CEV, NLT, and *The Message*. Hand out paper and pens. Assign groups one or more of the following Scriptures: Romans 6:1-4; Romans 6:5-8; Romans 6:9-11; Romans 6:12-13.

Say: "In your groups, I'd like you to look at all of the different translations, then see if you can figure out exactly what your part of the passage is saying. Then when you think you know what it means, write it in your own words *as if you were explaining it to a friend.*

To help you out, I have some hints. Come get them if you need them. I'll give you one at a time. Read it and see if it helps you figure things out any better before you ask for another. But see if you can figure things out with as few hints as possible."

Give the youth several minutes to work on their explanations, giving the hints out as necessary. When everyone has finished, read a portion of

Walk in Newness of Life

---

look for life

If you have more than eight people in your class, have them work in larger groups to save time.

Supplies: copies of page 54 cut apart, several copies of several versions of the Bible, paper, pens

If you don't have access to a number of different Bible translations, you'll find many of them online. One good source is *biblegateway.com*.

the Scripture and then ask the group to tell you what they decided it means. Continue until all groups have reported.

Say: "Wow! You did a great job of making sense of this really hard passage. So, now let's shrink it down even farther. What exactly does this whole 'newness of life' thing mean for us?" Ask for a volunteer to sum it up in a sentence or two.

AND

Perfected Blunders (6–8 minutes)

Supplies: large container, smaller container, sand, student journals, pens or pencils

If possible, get a large container (such as a small pool or a wagon) with enough sand for each person to have a large handful. Place the container in a corner of the room, but leave enough space for people to surround it. Also put some sand in a separate container such as a coffee can.

Sit around the sand. Ask:

- "What are some of the evidences that we live in a sinful world?

As people share their ideas, write them in the sand. After you have a few, take the other container of sand and slowly dump it on top of the words, covering them up.

Say: "These things, for us, are now buried by what Christ has done. They no longer need to be a part of our way of living."

Individually have the youth fill out the page in the student journal entitled "Perfected Blunders" (page 28). Give them a couple of minutes to read the poem and answer the questions. Ask them to work only on that page.

Bring the group back together around the sand, and ask them to take a big handful.

Say: "I want you to imagine all of your blunders in your life piled up. As I read the next Scripture, imagine Jesus taking care of your blunders. Let the sand slowly run out of your hands and believe that you can live a new life."

Read aloud Philippians 1:6 twice.

go with god

The Next Step (5–9 minutes)

Supplies: student journals, pens or pencils

Hand out the student journals and have the youth complete pages 29–31. Play some soft music in the background to help the students focus. Give them about 3–4 minutes to work, then let them know that they can take the journals home (if this is your final week of this issue in the series).

Ask:

- We've come to the end of the *Walk the Talk* issue. What are some of the things you remember having learned over the past seven weeks?

Briefly review the past few weeks with the youth. They might glance through their journals to help them remember some of their "Next Step" commitments. Close with a prayer in which each person adds a one-sentence prayer for God's help in walking the talk in one of the areas the group has studied.

Walk the Talk

Repro Page

Differing Results

Scripture	What are the results of humility?	What are the results of pride?
Proverbs 11:2		
Proverbs 13:10		
Proverbs 15:33		
Proverbs 16:5		
Proverbs 16:18		
Proverbs 18:12		
Proverbs 29:23		

Session 1 Reproducible Page

Permission is granted to photocopy this page for use in groups studying MAN WITH A MISSION. © 2003 by Abingdon Press.

Repro Page

What I Am Hearing

Record a bit of what you are hearing. What stories do the mentors tell? Record any profound or just plain funny things they say. Be sure to write down who said it.

More Questions (Record any additional questions you want to be sure to ask the mentors.)

I'm Learning (Use this section to record anything you are learning from the process.)

The Rubber Meets the Road

(Think about how you will use the things you are hearing today. Write about anything you need to do after listening to these mentors. You may want to spend some time later this week looking for more ways to apply what you have learned today.)

The Spiritual Side

(What do these mentors have to say about spiritual things? What have these mentors taught you about God and your faith?)

Session 5 Reproducible Page

Permission is granted to photocopy this page for use in groups studying MAN WITH A MISSION. © 2003 by Abingdon Press.

Scenarios

Scenario 1: Your sister, who is a year younger than you, has just come home crying hard because her friends have just said incredibly mean things to her. No one else is home, and you were just on your way out the door to go meet your friends. What should you do?

Scenario 2: It's the start of a new school year, and this year there are several new kids starting who had been home schooled previously. Everyone in your school is pretty tight because you've known one another for years. The new kids are finding it hard to fit in, because their experiences have been so different. What might you do to help them?

Scenario 3: You're with a friend playing Sardines (which is similar to Hide and Seek) in the dark during a church lock-in. While you're hunting for the person who hid, you notice a strange smell in one of the basement classrooms. You turn the light on to investigate and find a dirty, unkempt woman with two bags of personal items. What would you say to her? What could you do?

Scenario 4: You've just been elected vice-president of your school's student council. The president is someone you've never gotten along with. In fact, you find her to be arrogant and snobbish. She passes you in the hallway and rather rudely tells you that she wishes that you hadn't been elected. What would you say to her?

Scenario 5: Your dad has just lost his job, and the job market is pretty tight. He doesn't think that he'll be able to get a new job for a while, and the family can't make it on only your mom's salary for long. Everyone is the family is asked to think about ways to cut expenses. How could your faith help you to deal with the situation?

Scenario 6: Everyone in your youth group at church is really close to one another. A couple of weeks ago, you started dating one of the other youth in the group. But at the school dance this week, you broke up (and not by your choice). All of your friends at church know about everything and are pretty angry at your former date. How will you deal with being together at youth group next Sunday?

Scenario 7: Some of your friends have been dying to see a new movie that is out this weekend, and you have to admit that you'd like to see it too. But you know that it's filled with a lot of sexual jokes, crude stereotypes of ethnic minorities and women, and foul language. How will you deal with your friends when they call to plan when you're going to go see it?

Session 6 Reproducible Page

Bible Passages

Matthew 8:1-4

Lepers were people with skin diseases, and they were considered to be ritually unclean and thus untouchable. They were excluded from the community in every way. What does this passage tell you about Jesus?

Matthew 9:10-13

Tax collectors were strongly disliked because they had a reputation for being dishonest. "Sinners" could have been various people who were believed to be morally impure. What kind of people did Jesus choose to hang out with?

Matthew 9:35-38

Shortly after this story, Jesus sent out the disciples to share in his mission. What quality did he have and show that we, as his disciples, are now to imitate?

Matthew 12:1-8

Jewish Law forbade working on the Sabbath. One exception was that priests were allowed to perform sacrifices on that day, so they could legally break the law. Sacrifices and the Sabbath were two of the most important things for Jews. What does Jesus say is even more important?

Session 6 Reproducible Page

Permission is granted to photocopy this page for use in groups studying MAN WITH A MISSION. © 2003 by Abingdon Press.

Repro Page

Matthew 18:1-5
Adults often worry about their status in the world, but children do not. This was certainly true of Jesus' disciples and of the religious leaders of Jesus' day. What was Jesus' radical message to the disciples?

Matthew 18:21-35
The number 7 at that time implied completeness or doing something fully. What do these two stories tell you about the kind of person Jesus was?

Mark 10:17-27
Many of Jesus' stories and parables have to do with money. It's near the top of the list of subjects he talks about most. Why would Jesus think that money jeopardizes our spiritual health? What was his greater priority?

Luke 4:42-44; 5:15-16
Again and again, Jesus leaves everyone behind to go off by himself, especially after he has been with crowds of people. What was the source of his strength and renewal?

Luke 22:24-27
Jesus was known as a great teacher and a great healer, and many hoped that he would be a great leader. But what was Jesus' definition of what makes someone great?

Session 6 Reproducible Page

Permission is granted to photocopy this page for use in groups studying MAN WITH A MISSION. © 2003 by Abingdon Press.

Bible Tips

Romans 6:1-4
Tip 1: One of the things Paul was discussing in the previous chapter is if Christians should keep on sinning to experience more of God's grace, which means kindness and forgiveness.

Romans 6:1-4
Tip 2: In Paul's time, nearly all Christians were baptized as adults. They understood this as "being baptized into Christ's death."

Romans 6:1-4
Tip 3: Baptism into Christ's death means we die to our old way of life before we were followers of Jesus. Then, as Christ rose to new life, we experience a new kind of life too.

Romans 6:8-11
Tip 1: In Paul's time, nearly all Christians were baptized as adults. They understood this as "being baptized into Christ's death." That's what it means to have "died with Christ."

Romans 6:8-11
Tip 2: Just as Jesus lived his life in close relation to God, we now should see ourselves as "alive to God in Christ Jesus."

Romans 6:8-11
Tip 3: Just as death has no power over Christ anymore, sin does not need to have power over us anymore.

Romans 6:5-7
Tip 1: In Paul's time, nearly all Christians were baptized as adults. They understood this as "being baptized into Christ's death." Since Christ was resurrected, naturally we can expect to experience new life too.

Romans 6:5-7
Tip 2: When Christ died, our old, self-centered way of life died too. We don't have to be slaves to sin anymore.

Romans 6:5-7
Tip 3: Because of our baptism, we don't have to sin anymore. It's possible to live like slaves who have now been freed.

Romans 6:12-13
Tip 1: We have to choose not to let sin rule over us any more.

Romans 6:12-13
Tip 2: Because of our new life following our baptism, we must not use our bodies for doing wicked things but instead must use them for a new way of living.

Romans 6:12-13
Tip 3: Our new way of life-the only way of life that makes sense-is a life of righteousness, a life as tools that can be used for God's purpose in the world.

Session 7 Reproducible Page

Permission is granted to photocopy this page for use in groups studying MAN WITH A MISSION. © 2003 by Abingdon Press.

Repro Page

Get Walking

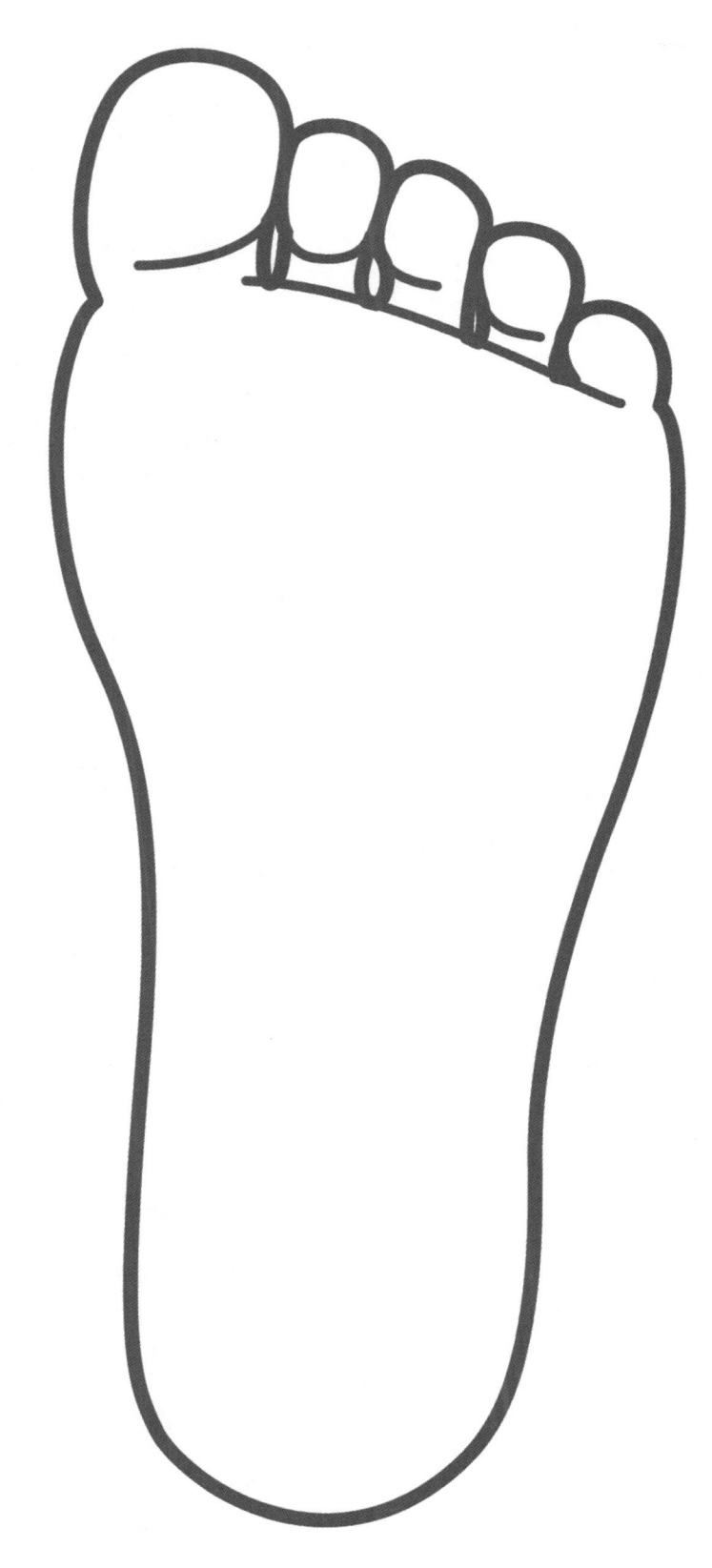

Retreat Reproducible Page

Permission is granted to photocopy this page for use in groups studying
MAN WITH A MISSION. © 2003 by Abingdon Press.

Road Signs

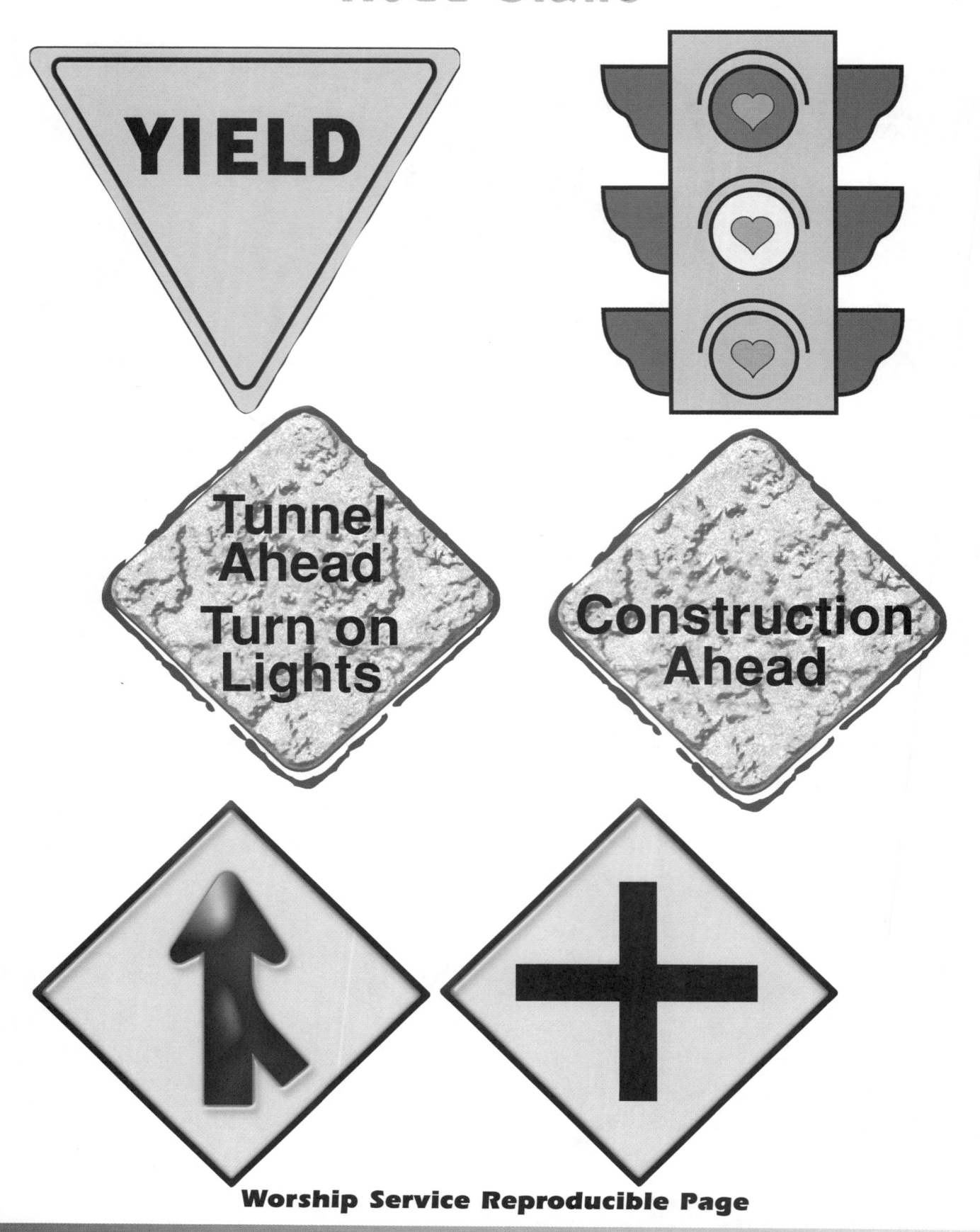

YIELD

Tunnel Ahead Turn on Lights

Construction Ahead

Worship Service Reproducible Page

Permission is granted to photocopy this page for use in groups studying MAN WITH A MISSION. © 2003 by Abingdon Press.

Walk With Jesus Retreat

"Walk a mile in my shoes; then you will understand."

What if your youth could walk in the sandals of Jesus? Use this retreat to help them "walk with Jesus." They will understand more about the life and love of Jesus. Ideally, use this retreat after completing the sessions.

S-H-O-E-S F-E-E-T is the acronym that sets the pattern for this retreat:

S—Simple beginnings
H—Hold it
O—Obedience
E—Eating
S—Surprise

F—Finished
E—Easter
E—Everyone
T—Transformed

Friday Night: Simple Beginnings

Mystery Meeting

Have everyone gather at the church with their personal belongings. Divide the youth so that you have a roughly equal number in each vehicle. Make sure that your adult drivers know the final destination, but encourage them not to tell. The drivers should also know the approximate time you want them to arrive at the mystery location. Each driver and youth needs to have a Bible.

Design a mystery course in which there are clues that lead to each new location, where the youth will find the next clue. Write these clues on paper stars; tell the youth that they will become the wise men and women.

At the stop before the final destination, have the driver read aloud **Matthew 2:1-11**. Then have the driver ask: "If you were going to meet Jesus tonight, what gift would you bring him?" After a brief discussion, the driver should say: "You are about to meet Jesus tonight. Spend the remainder of the trip in quiet, thinking about a gift you can give to Jesus."

As everyone arrives at the barn, have a "baby Jesus" lying in a manger. Hand out slips of paper and pens. Encourage the young people to write down the gift they want to give to Jesus and to place the slip beside the manger.

Invite the youth to pair with another person. Ask them to read **Luke 2:1-20** and talk about how the people in these verses responded to Jesus.

Say: "Join with another pair and answer this question: 'How have you responded to Jesus in your life?'"

Have your group gather around the manger. Ask: "If you were God and were going to come to earth, how might you do it? How was Jesus' birth an act of humility?"

A Walking Retreat

Leader Tip

If you don't have time for the entire retreat, choose the parts that fit your time and interests.

Also, to make the preparations easier, find a few assistants who can help plan a part of the retreat.

Leader Tip

Ideally, the destination should be a barn. If you are fresh out of barns in your area, try to arrange a special place at the retreat site. Use straw, a few stuffed toy animals, a "manger," and "baby Jesus."

Sample Schedule

Friday Night

7:00 Meet at church

7:45 Mystery site activities and campfire time

10:00 Snacks and unpack

11:30 Lights out

57

Leader Tip

You may want to have many copies of the foot page (page 55) on hand and let the youth periodically use them during the retreat to record their thoughts and impressions. Staple sheets of feet together as a booklet or put them in a folder for each youth so that they have a memory journal of the weekend.

If you cannot have a fire, hand out candles and start lighting them. If you cannot use candles, hand out flashlights.

Saturday Morning

8:00 Wake up call

8:30 Morning devotions: Hold It

9:15 Breakfast

10:00 Options: games, hiking, free time

12:00 Lunch

Invite a youth to read **Micah 6:8**. Then ask: "What have you been learning about walking in humility?"

Hand out copies of the foot page. Say: We'll be working with an acronym that will guide our retreat. We're ready for our first letter. Jesus came to earth with a *simple* beginning." Write the letter S on a large sheet of paper that you have posted on a wall or fence. You will eventually fill in the letters SHOES FEET, so be sure to leave enough room and fill in as you do the various activities.

Say: "Jesus gives us a wonderful example of what it means to be humble. Are there things in your life you could simplify? If there are, write them in the outline of one of the feet. Then get back with your partner and spend some time talking about how you could simplify your life."

While the youth are talking, quietly go to each pair and invite them to come outside into the dark. Encourage them to come in silence. Gather around an unlit fire. Ask: "How many of you don't like the dark? Why? How can God use darkness to help us see the light?"

Invite a youth to read **1 John 1:6.** Ask, "What are some things you remember about our study on walking in darkness?" Divide the youth into groups of three. Say: "Quietly talk about a time God has used the struggles in your life to help you." As they talk, light the fire.

When the fire is fully going, read aloud **Matthew 5:14-16**. Then have a youth read **John 8:12**. Ask: "What are the benefits of walking in the light? What are some times when it has been hard for you to walk in the light? Are there ways in which you have found it easier to walk in the light?"

While around the fire, your group can roast marshmallows and just enjoy the light. End the time with singing and prayer.

Saturday

Hold It

Wake up everyone, with a sign that says, "Silence. Be quiet while you get ready for the day." Your sign should also give them directions about when and where to gather for morning devotions and breakfast. When they arrive, have these questions written on large paper: "How many of Jesus' miracles took place before he was 30? How many sermons do we know about that he preached in his first 30 years of life? How easy or hard do you think it was for Jesus to wait? Why?"

After about 5 minutes of silence, whisper: "Spend the next few minutes quietly talking about what it is like to have to wait. Talk about whether you are good at waiting, and why or why not."

After a few minutes allow the group to talk aloud. Ask: "What was it like to be in silence for that long? Have you ever been told to wait until you're older to do something? Why would people tell you to wait until you are older? Why do you think Jesus waited until he was about 30 to begin his ministry? Do you ever feel as if you are waiting for something big to happen in your life? What is the hardest thing about waiting?"

Walk the Talk: In the Steps of the Soul Man

Say: "Many people talk about wanting to follow Jesus; yet when we look at his life, he did many things that are not a lot of fun." Have everyone pair up with someone different than the person they were with on Friday night. Invite a youth to read aloud **1 John 2:6**. Then talk about these questions: In what ways have you been walking as he walked? When is that easy for you? When is that hard to do?

Write the letter *H* on the appropriate large paper. Say: "Our next letter, stands for '*Hold* it.' Sometimes God asks us to hold it, to wait. Waiting was important in Jesus' life and for us when God tells us to wait."

Obedience

Gather around a river or other body of water. Read aloud **Matthew 3:13-17**. Talk with the youth about baptism. Ask questions such as, "Do you remember your baptism? What do you remember about it? What do you feel and think when there is a baptism during our church's worship services?"

Ask: "What does baptism mean?" (*It's a sign of our adoption by grace, a sign that we are incorporated into the church—the body of Christ, a promise of our faith and love in response to God's grace.*)

Hand out copies of your church's baptism liturgy, and read through parts of it with the youth. Ask: "Can you see places in this liturgy where obedience is a part of the service?" (*In the parent's agreement to bring a child up in faith; in the congregation's promise to support and nurture the parents and child; in the baptized person's commitment to a life of faith.*)

Say: "In the early church, people went through a lengthy study and preparation for baptism—typically a year. These "*chatecumens*" (CAT-uh-coom-ens) ended their study and joined the community through their baptism. Their intense study of the Christian faith was a sign of their obedience to Christ. *O* for *obedience* becomes our symbol."

Hold a baptismal renewal service. Invite a youth to read aloud **Romans 6:4**.

Spend the rest of the afternoon enjoying the water and one another.

The Last Supper

If possible, gather your group around the same table, or form a straight line of tables. If you have costumes, you can invite the youth to wear them to reenact the Last Supper. Read **Matthew 26:20**.

Toward the end of the meal, ask the youth to talk about these questions with those who are sitting around them: Talk about a time when your body was broken or bleeding—literally or figuratively. What did you want to happen? How well do you deal with pain? If you had the choice, would you go through it again?

Read aloud **Matthew 26:26-28**. Ask: "How much love did Jesus show by choosing to give up his body and his blood?"

Celebrate the sacrament of Communion together. Check with a pastor about your denomination's requirements for administering the sacrament.

A Walking Retreat

Saturday Afternoon

1:00 Baptism renewal

2:15 Water play and other options

Leader Tip

See your denomination's hymnal, book of worship, or your pastor for information about baptism renewal.

Talk with your pastor about this service and what is required. This is a time of remembering your baptism and renewing the vows; it is not the same as a baptism, which is ideally done within the church.

Saturday Early Evening

5:00 Reenact the Last Supper

6:30 Footwashing

Leader Tip

If your group is large, you may want to have a separate room in which to do the footwashing. Bring in small groups of youth at a time.

Read aloud **Romans 14:15** and **Ephesians 5:1-4.** Have the youth form pairs and talk about this question: "How easy or hard is it to walk in love?"

Say: "God wants us to eat, to partake of God's son. We can more fully love after we allow God to more fully love us. We now have the *E,* which stands for *eating*—the taking in of all that Jesus has done for us. We need to accept all that he has done for us. It is a free gift. If you are here tonight and have not made a decision for Christ, or if you simply wish to commit yourself more fully to a relationship with Jesus, please let me or one of the other leaders know. An important part of our faith is saying yes to Jesus and making a commitment to walking in his steps. (You may want to play a song and give a formal invitation.)

Footwashing

Read **John 13:5-15** together. Ask: "How was Jesus mentoring his disciples? What lesson was Jesus trying to teach his disciples?"

Say: "Jesus is full of surprises! He did something remarkable that night—something that you would not expect him to do. Yet that is just like love—so full of surprises. And we have our next letter, *S,* which stands for *surprises*. Let's read about a surprise Jesus had for his disciples."

Along with the other adult helpers, wash the feet of each youth. Ask: "How did it feel to have us wash your feet? What do you think we are saying by this action? How can Jesus be your mentor in life?"

Finished

Take the youth to a secluded, dark place. You may even want to blindfold them and lead them to the area. Read aloud **John 18:1-11.**

In small groups, let them talk about times when they have been betrayed or let down by others, and even by God. Ask, "What do you do when you are scared? What do you do when you are hurt?" Assign small groups one (or more) of the following Scriptures: **John 18:12-27; John 18:28-40; John 19:1-15; John 19:16-30; John 19:31-42.**

Instruct each group to prepare a way to tell their part of the story—read it, reenact it, make symbols, and so forth. However they choose to present their message, everyone in the group must be involved. Give them about 10 minutes to prepare, and then let each group present their message.

Have the group make a cross out of branches they find and take turns experiencing carrying it. Together, raise the cross. Read aloud **John 15:13.** Ask: "What does the cross have to do with the Christian walk?"

Read aloud **John 19:30.** Ask: "What did Jesus mean when he called out, 'It is finished'?"

Say: "We now have the next letter, *F*—for *finished*. Jesus' lived unconditionally for others, and his death was the ultimate symbol of God's unconditional love for us. Spend the next several minutes in silence before the cross. Listen for God. God wants you to learn something that will help improve your walk." Periodically break the silence by reading

---

Leader Tip

You'll need basins of warm, somewhat soapy water and several towels.

Saturday Late Evening

10:00 Finished

11:30 Lights out

Walk the Talk: In the Steps of the Soul Man

aloud **Romans 5:8; Romans 6:23; Ephesians 2:8-9; Galatians 2:20; Romans 10:11; Romans 8:35-39; Romans 3:23-24; Luke 14:27.**

Ask: "What do you need to do now? Spend a few minutes writing your thoughts; then with another person or two, discuss what you have written. Say: "For now, we are finished; but there is more. There is always more."

Sunday

Easter

Gather in a cemetery at sunrise. Talk about feelings about being there. Ask: "What makes you feel most alive? What scares you most about death?"

Read aloud **John 20:1-29.** Say: "Many people have claimed that they were God. Many people have asked others to follow them. But only one person who has ever claimed to be a son of God has risen from the dead."

Read aloud **John 11:25.** Say: "This is the promise we have. We usually refer to this promise as *Easter*. It is our hope. It is the next letter in the acronym we've been working with, the letter *E*. Without it, we have no hope. With it we can experience eternal life." Invite persons to give their testimony.

Ask everyone to answer this question in small groups: "How does Jesus' resurrection help us with our walk?" End this time with songs of praise.

Everybody

Read aloud **Matthew 25:31-46.** Say: "In your original car groups, figure out ways you could help people. Your group will have the next two hours to help as many people as you can. There are some rules. First, your adult sponsor must approve whatever you do. Second, you cannot spend any money helping them. If you need some sort of supply, use your ingenuity to come up with it as best you can. Third, whoever you help needs to know that you are helping them because Jesus loves them." Have the groups meet a designated place for lunch and sharing about their adventures.

Ask: "Where did you find Jesus? How did you help him?" Say: "All that Jesus did was to help each of us walk as he walked."

Read **Acts 26:20.** Say: "This gospel is for everyone, no matter where they are from. Thus we have the next letter, *E*, because *everyone* is included! No matter what, Christ's love is for everyone. Spend some time thinking about how you could help people in your life this week. When you have a list, talk about it with another person. Encourage one another to follow through."

Transformed

Read aloud **Romans 12:1-2.** Say: "Walking in the sandals of Christ will transform us. So we have the final letter, *T*, which stands for *transform*." In small groups, read **Romans 12:9-21** and **Ephesians 4:17-5:10.** Have the youth write on their foot paper practical answers to this question: "How will you be transformed by this retreat?" Dismiss with a favorite song and prayers.

A Walking Retreat

Leader Tip

You may want to get with a few of the youth who are articulate about their faith and ask them to prepare a testimony for tomorrow morning.

Sunday

Sunrise: Easter

Breakfast and pack up

9:30 Everybody assignment

12:00 Meet for lunch and Everybody debrief

1:00 Transformed

1:15 Dismiss

Leader Tip

The most convenient meeting place for lunch may be back at church so that the youth can meet their families. Have someone there ready with pizza or other lunch fare. You may wish to invite family members to lunch as well.

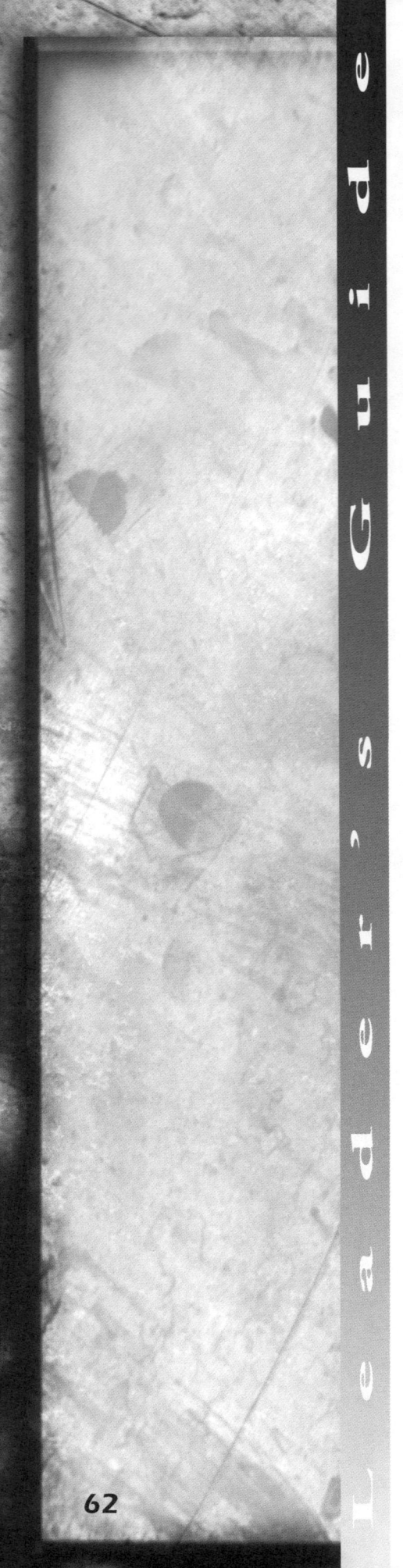

Out and About: Walking for Jesus

So far as we know, Jesus did all of his traveling on foot. All of the good news he brought to people didn't come by mail, e-mail, radio, or phone—it came by foot! Work with the youth in your class to pick a walking-related project you can tackle together as a way of bringing good news to others. Here are some examples:

- Get sponsors for a walk-a-thon for a mission project you all want to support.

- Have a "Dog Walk Weekend" in which your group agrees to walk people's dogs twice each day for a donation. Some animal shelters also welcome volunteer dog walkers.

- Walk along the roads of your community and pick up trash. Be sure to keep safety in mind when choosing a location.

- Find a church or retreat center in your area that has a labyrinth and spend an hour walking it in silence and prayer.

- Design a flyer advertising your church, then walk around town and deliver it to people's houses.

- Invite a youth group from a nearby church to meet you for a picnic halfway between your locations. Be sure to encourage both groups to walk to the picnic.

- Do some research into how far people in many parts of the world have to walk to find clean, safe water. Walk that distance together to get a feel for how far that is, and talk about ways you can help raise funds for rural well projects abroad.

- Do the mission project near the end of the retreat (see "Everybody," page 61) for another idea, which could include walking.

Walk the Talk: In the Steps of the Soul Man

Worship Service: Walk in God's Ways

Gather a short distance from the worship space. When everyone has arrived, say: "The most common phrase in the Bible associated with the word *walk* is 'Walk in God's ways.' Again and again, the people of Israel were told to know God's ways, to walk in them, and to not stray from God's way. During this service, you'll have a chance to think about what it means to walk in God's ways and to commit yourself to walking in the way of the Lord. As we walk to our worship space, I encourage you to silently prepare yourself for worship."

Walk together to the place where you've planned to hold the service. Say: "Before we were even aware of it, God was walking with us. Even at the end of life, God will still walk with us. In between these times, our call is to walk in God's ways. Let's sing together the song that will be the theme for this service, 'Step by Step.'"

Sing the song twice through so that anyone who is unfamiliar with the song can learn it.

Ask one of the youth to read aloud **Psalm 119:1-10**, or read it in unison as a group. (Use a version such as the NRSV, which in verse 9 contains the words *young people*.)

Say: "Psalm 119 is the longest psalm in the Bible. In fact, it's the longest chapter in the Bible. It's a song all about the ways and laws of God. By the time it is done, eight different terms are used for God's ways: *commandments, statutes, ordinances, decrees, words, precepts, promises,* and *laws.* The psalmist loves to meditate on the laws of God found in Scripture and hopes that he will steadily keep going in God's ways. In the song, we sang that we will follow God one step at a time—that's the only way we can walk by faith. In each moment, we have a decision to make—will I continue to walk in the ways of God or in the ways of someone else? But what are the ways of God? The Jews had 587 laws to follow, but Micah summed them up in just a few words."

Have another youth read aloud **Micah 6:8.** Then say, "I've asked some of you to tell a story that relates to the six themes we'll look at today. The first theme is walking humbly. (Insert the name of the youth), will you tell us your story?"

Sing "Step by Step" again. Say: "Walking humbly means we remember that we must give God the control of our lives."

Hand out the copied road signs and ask, "The first road sign for our journey of faith is the yield sign. What does it mean to yield our lives to God?"

Supplies: Bible; a set of road signs (page 56) cut apart for each person; words and music for "Step by Step," by Rich Mullins

Leader Tip

Before the service, find six volunteers to share a story from their life related to one of the following: walking humbly with God, walking in love, walking in darkness and in the light, walking with a spiritual friend, walking as Jesus walked, walking in newness of life. If you are unable to find someone else from the group or from the congregation to share a story, you may choose to do this yourself.

Many praise chorus books or contemporary hymnals will have the song, "Step by Step," by Rich Mullins.

If possible, hold this service in a park, forest, or other area where the youth can walk in silence during a part of the service.

Worship Service: Walk in God's Ways

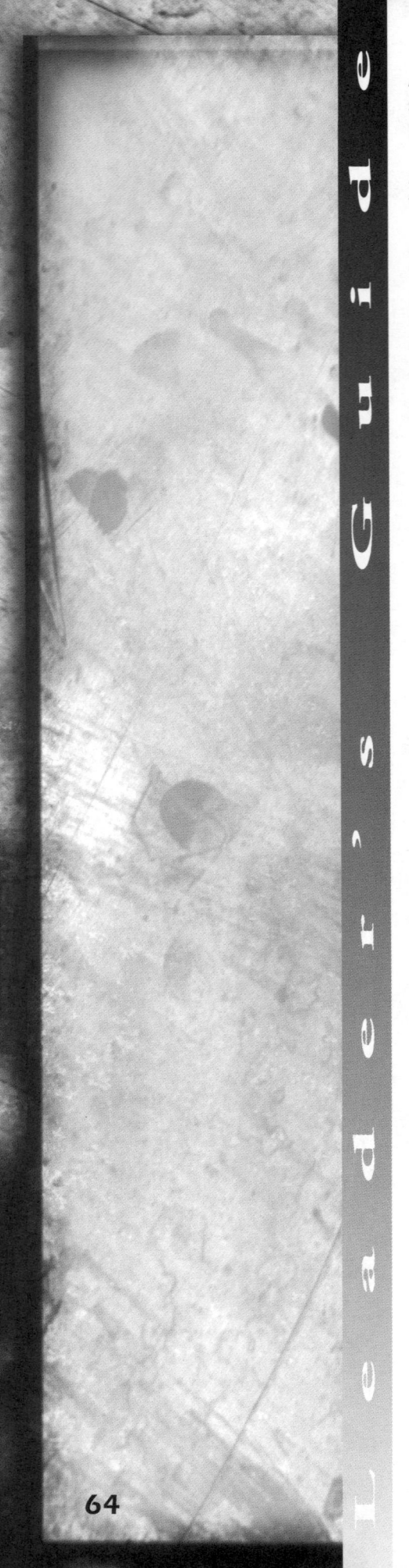

Allow a few youth to answer, then hand out pens. Say: "On your yield sign, write a word or two about a part of your life that you need to humbly yield to God."

Ask a youth to read aloud **Ephesians 5:1-2,** then have the second volunteer tell his or her story about walking in love. Sing the song again.

Have the youth the traffic light. Say: "We usually call this a traffic light or "stoplight," but I'd like for you to think of it as a 'go light.' On your go light, write a way that you will go out and love others in Jesus' name."

Continue the rest of the service with the same pattern: Scripture, story, song, sign, as follows:

3. **1 John 2:7-11.** "We are so often surrounded by darkness that it can feel as if we're entering a dark tunnel. The best thing we can do when surrounded by darkness is to turn on our light. On your tunnel sign, write a place where you need to let God's light shine through you."

4. **Luke 24:12-16, 30-32.** "Our journey of faith is never one we undertake alone. There are always others to walk with us. The construction ahead sign reminds us that our faith is always growing and changing, and it is through the help of others that much of that change occurs. On your sign, write the name of a friend who you can help as they walk their journey of faith."

5. **1 John 2:6.** "When we have trouble knowing which way to go, the way of Jesus will always be a truth that will lead us. The merge sign reminds us that our way must merge with Jesus' way. On your merge sign, write the words 'my way' on the side road and 'His way' on the main road."

6. **Proverbs 12:28.** "Our final sign is a crossroads, for that's where we find ourselves. Will we take the road of righteousness and the way of the cross, or will we turn back and go another way? The cross on this sign reminds us that our new life in Christ requires love of God—that's the vertical line—and love of neighbor—the horizontal line. I'd like for you to take a walk now in silence for five minutes. As you walk, consider what direction you will go and where the road may lead you as you come to this intersection."

When everyone has returned, say: "Keep these road signs and put them up around your room or in your school locker to remind you of your commitments on your walk of faith. Let's close by singing the song one more time."

Join hands and close with the song.

Walk the Talk: In the Steps of the Soul Man